Children in the Way?

Children in the Way?

Creative opportunities for churches
with young children

Carrie Kingston
and
Isobel MacDougall

MONARCH
BOOKS

Oxford, UK & Grand Rapids, Michigan, USA

First published in the UK in 2011 by Monarch Books
(a publishing imprint of Lion Hudson plc)
Wilkinson House, Jordan Hill Road, Oxford OX2 8DR, England
Tel: +44 (0)1865 302750 Fax: +44 (0)1865 302757
Email: monarch@lionhudson.com
www.lionhudson.com

ISBN 978 0 85721 029 6 (print)
ISBN 978 0 85721 244 3 (epub)
ISBN 978 0 85721 243 6 (Kindle)
ISBN 978 0 85721 245 0 (PDF)

Distributed by:
UK: Marston Book Services, PO Box 269, Abingdon, Oxon, OX14 4YN
USA: Kregel Publications, PO Box 2607, Grand Rapids, Michigan 49501

Illustrations pages 14, 55, 56, 86 (child), 107, 108, 143, 144, 146, 169, 207, 208, 216 copyright © Rebecca Kingston 2011. Used with permission.
Illustrations pages 73, 86 (diagram): Lion Hudson
Poem pages 143–144 "What Did You Do at Pre-School Today?" © Sue Heard, Staffordshire Pre-school Learning Alliance. Used with permission.
Poem pages 54–57 "The Little Boy" by Helen E Buckley, first published in School Arts Magazine, October 1961. Used with permission.
Poem pages 106–107 "The 100 Languages of Children" by Loris Malaguzzi, Founder of the Reggio Emilia Approach, translated by Lella Gandini © Preschools and Infant-toddler Centers – Instituzione of the Municipality of Reggio Emilia, Italy, published by Reggio Children. Used with permission.

British Library Cataloguing Data
A catalogue record for this book is available from the British Library.

Printed and bound in Malta by Gutenberg Press.

We dedicate this book to our children and grandchildren, who have inspired us and provoked us to rethink creatively about children.
So here's to:
Naomi Davis, James, Rebeca and Abigail MacDougall, Lily and Noah Davis, Josh and Rebecca Kingston.

Contents

Acknowledgments

We would like to acknowledge all those people we have worked with over the years who have shaped our beliefs about children – including the children we have taught, engaged with and been inspired by.

We would also like to thank those who have helped us to write this book: for proofreading, especially Bill and Abi MacDougall; for creative ideas and illustrations, especially Rebecca Kingston. A special thank you to Alan Mann for his encouragement to get started… and to keep going! And to Kairen Smith, our educational consultant.

Most of all we want to thank our families. Huge thanks to Neil and Bill for their encouragement, tolerance, patience, cups of tea and belief in us. Also to our children who gave us the original idea and the motivation to write this book in the first place, and who have been some of our greatest teachers. They have made us think outside the box, helped us to reflect, caused us to seek God in new ways and opened our perceptions of God as parent. So, heartfelt thanks to James, Naomi, Rebeca and Abi, Josh and Rebecca.

Lastly, we would like to acknowledge each other for the fantastic experience of writing together! Coming from very different places, we have established an enriching and enjoyable creative partnership.

Preface

A long time ago…

Well, not so long ago, on a journey to work at the same university, this conversation began. As we shared our own individual stories we discovered we shared a desire to make a difference for the very youngest children in church. We found that although our professional backgrounds came from different places, we shared a similar ethos and philosophy. So this dialogue evolved through friendship, through debate, through long discussions – our differences acting as a catalyst for further exploration.

And so we began to write.

We invite you to join in this organic process of thinking through your beliefs and values for our youngest children. Throughout this book we have questioned our thinking, challenged our assumptions, reflected on our practice and tussled with ideas and research. We have searched for the principles that are embedded in the Bible and expressed in glimpses with Jesus.

Now we invite you to join us and do the same.

We have provided plans and ideas for children's groups; however, you need to consider the foundations which are articulated in this book, providing the principles for the building blocks, before you use the plans.

We recommend that you record your reflections (your thoughts and questions) in a journal, talk through your thinking with others or if you wish to, contact us through our website: www.childrenintheway.com

This book is all about relationships and reflections on how we relate to very young children. It begins with an overview of children in the twenty-first century and identifies changes that have taken place in recent years, as well as considering what life may be like for our children in the future. Section 3 then focuses on children under three, considering what the best-quality care may look like for these children, including an appropriate environment and the role of the people who care for them. Section 4 describes the rich resources for children aged three to seven years and highlights the importance of relationships, quality materials and the power of stories.

As we look at our churches today, are children in the way? Is this what God is saying about the place of children? When our church children grow up, will they still be walking in "the way" because they have enjoyed their experience of church and felt the love of God expressed to them through their contact with the important adults at church?

Our motivation for writing this book came out of our concern that children are being short-changed in church and we need to make a positive change for them and more importantly, with them.

So surely, now is the time to change!

Ecclesiastes 3:1–11

A Time for Everything

There is a time for everything,
and a season for every activity under the heavens:
A time to be born and a time to die,
A time to plant and a time to uproot,
A time to kill and a time to heal,
A time to tear down and a time to build,
A time to weep and a time to laugh,
A time to mourn and a time to dance,
A time to scatter stones and a time to gather them,
A time to embrace and a time to refrain from embracing,
A time to search and a time to give up,
A time to keep and a time to throw away,
A time to tear and a time to mend,
A time to be silent and a time to speak,
A time to love and a time to hate,
A time for war and a time for peace…

…He has made everything beautiful in its time.
He has also set eternity in the human heart.

Church Through a Child's Eyes

This section will seek to explore aspects of church from a child's perspective and will pose reflective questions. The main themes of the book will be introduced, including current scientific studies and how children learn. This section is rooted in Christian beliefs.

CHAPTER 1

Time Flies

Isobel

In 1956, in a Sunday School in Sheffield, I remember standing singing "Somewhere beyond the blue, there's a mansion for me…" I had no idea what it meant, and for years I wondered where "the blue" was. As for the mansion, I am still waiting for it to materialize! Sunday School was held every week at 3.00 p.m. to evangelize children and teach them about the Christian faith, and from an early age I went with my siblings.

Was this education or entertainment?

I would suggest it was neither, but it did occupy us for the afternoon and give our parents some respite; not that this was the intention.

Sunday Schools were originally started in Gloucester in 1780 by Robert Raikes to educate poor children from the factories. Children were taught from the Bible how to read and write, and developed their memory by learning passages of the Bible by heart. These children were working during the week, with no opportunity to attend school. Sunday Schools provided the opportunity for them to learn to read and write and also gave their parents, who were also working throughout the week, time to do their household chores and prepare for the next week. This was of course a time when many people in the UK attended church regularly, and social action was high on the agenda, so educating poor children was perceived as a valuable charitable act.

As time went on, and education for all children became compulsory, these afternoon Sunday Schools evolved to teach children about God and to evangelize children who were not from Christian families. When I was in Sunday School in Yorkshire in the 1950s, we used to go on marches through the town with a large banner, to recruit new members.

Sunday Schools gradually moved into the morning service and the tradition of children "going out" to their church groups developed. The expression "Sunday School" disappeared, to be replaced by more "user-friendly" terms, since the purpose of the "school" was no longer to educate children to read and write. These groups now tend to be for the children of families attending church. But has the ethos of a formal school lived on in our practice?

So, did my experience of Sunday School do me any harm?

Well, yes it did. It inoculated me against any interest in or enjoyment of church.

Of course, it wasn't *just* Sunday School. Sitting through boring services in the morning added to my dislike of Sundays, a dislike which continued into adulthood, as I quickly found the content irrelevant to my own life and experience. Is it any surprise that teenagers have left the church in droves? What is there to hold their interest and attention?

Clearly times have changed. Very few churches hold an afternoon Sunday School. Children's church is now an integral part of the life of the church. Or is it? Is it genuinely integral to the life of the church, or just an addition?

This book is designed for church leaders, leaders of children's groups, children's and youth workers in churches and anyone else who is interested in finding out more about the needs of very young children (i.e. from birth to seven years), and practical ways to work with them.

Some readers may belong to big churches where you have large groups of children and several teams of leaders. Others will belong to a smaller church and may have a few children across a wide age range and only one leader. Whatever your context, we hope that you will be able to find some helpful information, useful strategies and good resources which will support you in your work with children.

In 2010 I stayed on holiday in a medieval town in France with Evie, aged two years, and Niall, aged eight months. Evie was delighted with the clock tower at the end of the lane which struck the hour twice each hour, and the ancient church a few metres from our house. Every day Evie wanted to visit the church several times. As we entered the church she would tell me that we needed to be quiet, then she said that we could pray for mummy and daddy. As we went down the nave she would utter a small scream, which I would imitate, followed by a louder one and the exasperated comment, "It doesn't do it, Granny." I would reply, "No, it doesn't have a good echo".

Evie loves church. She attends most weeks with her parents and loves the singing and watching all the people and meeting up with friends. She attends crèche and loves it best when Daddy is there. She clearly sees church as a fun place to be where she can express herself. As she negotiated the new experience of the darkened church in France, with its candles and statues of saints, it was interesting that she was initially anxious and clung to me hard. She sensed the need for silence, but as the medieval church became more familiar to her on our repeated visits, she became more courageous and able to test the resonance of the building. Was it significant that the previous day she had been in the tunnel through the castle with her mother and they had listened for echoes?

At the age of two, Evie is an explorer, a scientist, an investigator of her world using all the knowledge she has acquired as well as her senses to develop the images in her brain, and repetition helps to make these brain connections strong.

Niall loved the church for a very different reason. He loved to crawl and pull himself up until he was standing on the pews. Using his thumbs to test out the texture and feel of objects and surfaces, he squealed with delight with his freedom to explore the church, freed from the restraints of the buggy! Niall used the senses he was born with to find out about his world. He was very sensitive to changing atmospheres as well as textures, temperatures, smells and sounds. Everything was tested by mouth. Niall is reliant on these senses and the mouth has many nerve endings which feed the brain with information – is the object hard, soft, smooth, rough, hot or cold? Is it edible?

In recent years, brain research has provided us with valuable information about very young children. We know that from their earliest moments, babies are able to imitate actions by others and their brains are stimulated by positive touch and affection. Care and attention from a few known and trusted adults will help the synapses in the brain to develop rapidly, and the baby needs conversation, touch and contact with people in order to thrive. Although there are many gurus and guidebooks to inform and confuse parents and carers, one thing is clear through brain studies – love really does matter!

So how do we respond to this new research in our churches?

The first few years of a child's life are arguably the most important time of their lives. These years lay the foundations for their future. They are crucial years and they disappear fast! Ask any parent. Time flies!

What do we provide for our youngest children and why?

When it comes to young children, is our primary purpose as churchgoers to provide a safe place for babies so that parents can worship, or is it to provide a place that gives babies particular messages about themselves? If very young children need consistent care from familiar caregivers with whom they can form an attachment, why do we staff our crèches with a rota of people? We seem to think that adults are the ones who need continuity and expertise, so they are taught and led by the same qualified leaders each week!

Why?

Are we more concerned about the adults' need to learn and grow spiritually?

Young children are experiential learners. They learn through doing and discovering. Evie loves books, and has done so since she was about six months old. Niall likes to move about and at the time of writing shows little interest in books, except eating them! Whatever their interests, children need a variety of activities. Do you remember *Sesame Street* – the children's TV programme which was always based on a letter, a number and a concept, and then for an hour had cartoons, stories and questions based on these? As a primary school teacher and a university lecturer, I use this principle for teaching and it seems to work for all ages.

Evie loves to have stories either read or told to her, and enjoys the familiarity of the same story over and over again. These stories are about people and / or animals in relationships having an adventure together. The Bible is full of interesting stories about life experiences which are familiar to young children, and these are great sources for children's church groups – but not for an hour! More like three to five minutes – then it is time to play with sand and water, or run around with bikes and trucks and imaginary play resources. What about providing props in a Story Sack or Box and then leaving these props for the children to re-enact the story at their own leisure?

But will the children remember the story? Will we be wasting their "church" time?

Children have phenomenal memories for detail.

> Lying on the bed with a child aged two and a half, I pretended to be asleep in the hope that she would go to sleep, but was enthralled as she told her bear the story "Going on a Bear Hunt", with all the intonation, variety of volume, pace and accuracy of the book. She knew it, she understood it and she felt it!

Throughout his earthly life, Jesus used stories to teach people how to live and relate to God and the world.

Why?

Stories allow us to imagine and think freely. They provide us time to process our thoughts, relate the story to our own story, repeat the events and understand the concepts within a context. One of my favourite stories in the New Testament is the woman who lost a coin. I can identify with the loss of something of great emotional value. I lost my wedding ring many years ago. It had been made for us by a friend and we had gone to choose the gold and the design at his studio in Hatton Garden.

I have also seen the beautiful headdresses that Jewish women used to wear when they got married, made up of coins. I have lived in fairly dark, basic accommodation where it is dusty and easy to lose a coin and where sweeping is the only way to find something on the floor. Consequently, this story resonates with me and I can feel the anxiety of the loss followed by the exhilaration on finding the coin.

So telling stories to young children rather than exploring abstract themes is appropriate. Over time they will begin to make connections with the biblical significance contained in the story – but not yet.

Surely stories are not appropriate for babies?

Well, babies do love stories but they also need plenty of sensory experiences. They need activities such as singing and finger rhymes, which are valuable for language acquisition; also they need a few well-chosen bought toys that provide a variety of options, such as stacking cups and wooden blocks. Elinor Goldschmied[1] designed Treasure Baskets based on her observations and research with very young children. She noticed that these children liked to explore through their senses to learn about the world. Treasure Baskets contain a range of natural resources such as fir cones, wooden blocks, cotton reels and spoons which are stored in a basket which is placed in front of a child aged six to twelve months (as soon as the child can sit with support). The child explores the items in the basket independently, without the involvement of the adult. The adult's role is to ensure that the child is safe and content. I would suggest that any crèche should have several baskets, each of which could have a different theme – e.g. one of wooden objects, one of metal etc.

Creativity is at the heart of all learning.

We are all creative, and given the opportunities in life, we will explore, invent, imagine, hypothesize and make decisions for ourselves.

So, are all children independent thinkers and decision makers? Yes, to the degree that they are able. It is appropriate to give them some control over their learning; after all, we all learn best when we are interested and motivated to find out more about things. Article 17 of the United Nations Convention of Rights for the Child (1989) suggests that children should have the right to make choices and have a say in actions and decisions which involve them. It is my belief that children's rights concur with biblical views on childhood. After all, Jesus himself both valued and respected children.

In recent years, early childhood educators have encouraged trainees to go back to the principles of pioneers such as Friedrich Froebel, Susan Isaacs and the MacMillan sisters, who advocated a child-centred approach to working with young children. Will this produce a child-centred universe where children have all they want and get their own way all the time? Won't we be left with a society of spoiled brats?

No, although there are people who fear this! This concept of child-centred practice means starting where the child is, with what they have experienced and what they already know, and ensuring that all care and learning is developmentally, culturally and socially appropriate for the child. In a child-centred approach we try to view the world through the eyes of a child, avoiding making assumptions about them based on our own experiences or knowledge of childhood. This does mean that we do not impose our adult views and beliefs on the young child. After all, children are highly sensitive and tune in to attitudes and atmospheres. They learn most from home and it is here that they develop spiritually and absorb the values and beliefs of their care-givers – through the way they are nurtured, shown affection and have their needs met. However, the way we respond to and provide for young children in the church will affect the way they view God, and our actions do speak louder than words.

Children's church: What is it for?

Or should we ask, *who* is it for? Unless we reflect on what we do, we may just repeat unthinkingly what was done to us in our childhood or what we assume should be done.

We are surrounded by books, television programmes and courses offering guidance on how to bring up children, but in our reflections on the place and purpose of children's church and crèches we need to focus on *why* we do what we do rather than just *how* we do it. I believe that the latter will naturally evolve when we have asked the former.

> As a part of my work, I visit many settings for children from the age of birth to eight years. I see a variety of practice; some children are engaged and intensely involved, some are merely occupied and some are just bored. Some of the environments are state-of-the-art, some are sparsely resourced and some are full of clutter. However, the most important resource is always the adults and their attitude, interest and skills. It is these people that actually make the difference for children. On one occasion I visited a nursery where seven babies were lined up in their high chairs being fed by two passive, silent adults. These babies were silent and non-responsive – already institutionalized.

Are we in danger of institutionalizing children to conform to the adult church in our desire to "feed" them Christianity?

Over the past ten years there have been many changes in attitudes towards working with the youngest children, based on research, a greater focus on early childhood education, and improved training. Research into the development of the brain, key relationships, infant mental health, the importance of play, the impact of physical movement, emotional development and access to the natural world, to name a few areas, have all generated positive changes in the provision for children and their families.

In addition, within the early childhood sector, we have also become more aware of the social issues that affect families such as poverty, disability, domestic violence and inequality. (The British "Sure Start" initiative was set up to address inequality and some churches have responded to the social divisions in the UK, which I believe is a vital part of the role of the church.)

We have become more aware of the multicultural nature of our society and the rich diversity that this offers communities. Many schools are multilingual and most of us benefit from the global nature of our shopping outlets, cafes and restaurants.

But what about Sundays?

Does what children experience in churches on Sundays reflect something of the advances in knowledge and understanding through current research in psychology and education and through globalization? What about our own cultures? Do we leave these at the door? What about the culture and language of Christianity: Hebrew? Patriarchal? Ancient? Jewish? Interpreting what it meant for people in Bible times is an important factor, but applying this to our own cultures needs careful consideration.

So how are we training our children's work team? Who is in our team?

Many churches are concerned with "doing church differently" to meet the needs of the current generation and the cultural mix within society – and rightly so.

The decline in church attendance is a clear indication that the old traditions are no longer working for everyone. As we study the different formats of "cafe church", emerging church and fresh expressions, have we thought about the children within these churches? I believe that this is where we need to start our thinking – with the children, from the roots of our society up, rather than from the top down, which is so often our educational model.

After all, it was Jesus who said, "Unless you change and become like little children…"[2] It is important to remember that when Jesus singled out children and put them in a position of importance, this was counter-cultural. Children were of little status in those times – along with women. A boy would be more important than a girl, so perhaps it is significant that Jesus selects "a child".

Our understanding of how children perceive the world, learn and develop has come on by leaps and bounds in recent years. Schools and other institutions working with children are constantly reviewing and adjusting their practices in line with the latest insights in order to give our children the best opportunities to learn and grow. And yet, most churches, which have the potential to change society and improve the lives of all children, all too often employ antiquated practices in their children's work.

Jesus said, "Let the little children come to me, and do not hinder them."[3] Unfortunately, even with the best of intentions, so many churches alienate children because our methods don't meet their developmental and cultural needs, and because we don't realize that some of the strongest messages we give them are the hidden ones.

Most churches claim to accept and value children. Some demonstrate this by having a children's corner, a box of books or toys in a remote area of the church, or by sending children out to Sunday School, children's church or a specific group. Others allow children to run around freely and to have free access to the building during services. Some do a mixture of both, depending on the week of the month.

- What message does this give to both adults and children?
- What do children learn about God and his kingdom?
- What do adults learn about the place and value of children?
- Is this really a rather lazy opt-out approach to welcoming families into church?

Recently, when I attended an all-age service, two young children ran around the church chasing each other. They squealed with the anticipation of being caught, and the adults looked on uncomfortably. I beckoned one child aged four to explore toys at the back of the church, and together we went out with our basket of prepared toys into the vestibule. The basket was full of parts of plastic toys, and two cars. We improvised a game and before long, most of the children in church had slipped out to join us. My point is this: had the children been engrossed in the service, they would have stayed. Even though the resources were poor, the opportunity to play with or engage with someone was more interesting. Although I was not on duty with the children, I do have a relevant CRB[4] check, which is always important.

- So, where does God come into this?
- What are our principles for children's church?

What about churches which have baptism services or dedication services for young children? How does the church manage the possible influx of visiting children who come with the baptism party? This may well be the child's first experience of church. The adult who accompanies the child into children's church may also feel uncomfortable in this context.

How do we, as children's church leaders, manage this? Are we primarily concerned about the impact on our "regular children" or more concerned about connecting with the visitors?

I have raised many questions and touched on a myriad different concepts within this chapter. We will be dealing with these in more detail throughout the rest of the book. We suggest that you keep a notebook to jot down your thoughts as you read and to record your responses to the "Reflections" at the end of each chapter.

Some of the currently available programmes for working with children in church are watered-down adults' materials, the focus of church being to teach adults. So what we are suggesting is radical in that we always start with the child, and build from there. This book will give you the research and reasoning that is the evidence for this practice.

You will notice the image of the dandelion throughout this book. Why have we chosen this? Many people, including my husband, think of the dandelion as a nuisance; just a weed which spreads through the garden quicker than you can get rid of it! Did you know that its name is a corruption of the French *dent de lion*, meaning "lion's tooth"? In the Old Testament, the lion is an image used for God, and God is the *raison d'être* for this book. Dandelion flowers are sensitive to light, so they open with the sun in the morning and close in the evening or during gloomy weather. They are attractive to young children because of their bright colour and also can be used medicinally for a wide range of conditions such as poor digestion, liver disorders, and high blood pressure. However, when the dandelion goes to seed and the "clocks" form, the seeds disperse and reproduce very effectively! You can interpret this symbol in many ways.

This beautiful flower, seen as a weed, is useful and fragile. Children can be seen as a nuisance, but they can teach us so much about life. Yet like the dandelion clock, we will lose children from the church if we fail to meet their needs.

Meet the authors

This is Isobel writing. I have spent all of my life within the church – and my involvement has varied! My parents were employed in Christian ministry and we moved frequently with their careers, so I experienced a variety of churches and children's groups. I have four adult children, two grandchildren and am married to a pastor. I was born in Nigeria, spent most of my childhood in England and then lived and worked with my husband and children in Argentina for three years. I started my career as a children's nurse and then I became a primary school teacher. My work now involves teaching an undergraduate degree to qualified, employed practitioners working within the whole range of contexts for young children and their families. I started working in children's church groups when I was fourteen years old as the leader of an Infant Sunday School. I had two staff younger than me and at least seventy children under eight years each week. I was determined that the children should enjoy their experience – based on my own variable experiences!

I love life, the natural world, my home, my friends and my family. I have learned so much through my children and grandchildren, and love being part of their lives, from newborn to adulthood. I also enjoy study, which is why at sixty I am still a student! My particular interest and expertise is the study of children from birth to three years within a particular social context, including bilingual cultures.

Hi, this is Carrie. My passion to make a positive difference for children led me into Early Years education after my degree in Physiology. I trained under an inspirational tutor and mentor, Peter Heaslip, who taught me an abiding respect for young children. My expertise in the education of children from three to seven years old began here and has developed throughout my working life.

During the early years of my marriage to Neil, a chartered accountant, I taught in an infant school and then had a rare opportunity of setting up a new nursery as part of a school. This gave me free rein to put into practice all that I held dear.

Later I left to have my two children, Josh and Rebecca, who are now in their twenties, and I began to experience children's church from both sides of the equation. This included various church plants and working in different buildings.

On returning to work in my professional life, in addition to more nursery teaching and working in children's church, I have also been a registered nursery Ofsted inspector, an Advisory Teacher for Early Years for Bristol and a college and university senior lecturer with a desire to provide the best quality for children wherever they are, through inspiring others.

I can't really believe it, but Neil and I have now been married for thirty years!

My own personal enthusiasms and where I connect most easily with

God are through wildlife, exploring new creative expressions and bizarrely, through participating in sport of all kinds.

More recently I have had an unexpected twist to my journey, with several back operations leading me to take early retirement on grounds of ill health. It has been a time of lovingly supportive family and friends, of knowing "God with me" and of waiting expectantly.

This book has been a dream discussed with Isobel during shared commutes to work and is now, to our joy, becoming reality. Who knows, but maybe I have come to this position "for such a time as this".[5]

Although we are co-writing this book, we hope that you will get to know us as individuals and hear our unique voices. We also hope that you will add your own voice to this book. We pose questions, raise issues, make suggestions and at times, hope to be provocative – and we hope that you will respond with your own unique thoughts and questions based on your experiences, education and beliefs.

Above all, we hope that as a result of this book, young children and their families will grow in their relationship with God.

We also hope you enjoy the marvel of recognizing the competence, creativity, originality and magic of each individual child as you allow them to share power with you and adopt a more child-centred approach, so that this next generation in your church will love being there and will want to remain connected to God throughout their lives.

Reflection

- What are the key questions for you in this chapter?
- Draw a time line from ten minutes before leaving the house to go to church, to ten minutes after you return home, and plot how much time your children (or your "church" children) are
  - *doing something on an adult's agenda.*
  - *have chosen something for themselves to do.*

CHAPTER 2

Just in Time?

I like that!

Carrie and Isobel

This is my place: a sense of belonging, part of the valued community, part of my identity

We are all unique individuals and we are all of equal value. The God of heaven and earth who bothered to make each snowflake with an individual pattern, who takes delight in giving each of us different fingerprints, most certainly takes joy in planting individuality in each and every one of us. He puts some of his characteristics in us as well.

Including children.

So, if we value each child as unique, we have to ensure that we allow them to be true to themselves. They need to be allowed the freedom of individuality and freedom of expression, within appropriate social contexts, not running wild but not trained like soldiers either.

Children need to feel that church is a place for them, that they have a sense of belonging. They need to feel that they are a valued member of that community, with a church family that provides quality time and has appropriate expectations of them. They need to be high on the church's agenda, as they are high on God's agenda. They might also be future leaders and are an important part of church growth.

Giving each child a badge, or having a welcome board for registration with the child's photograph, is a practical way of recognizing the membership and acceptance of that child within the group. Even the youngest children sense this.

Young children embrace the experiences they are given and accept that this is the way the world works. However, later, as they are able to make more evaluative judgments and maybe haven't felt that they fitted in or felt "good enough" in some way, then they will vote with their feet and opt out of church altogether. In effect they will have been "inoculated" against church or Christianity.

Will we be just in time to make positive changes for our youngest church children that could influence their perception of church and the relevance of God's love for them for the rest of their lives?

Children should be viewed as equal members of the church body. However, Jesus goes even further and says they are of special value:

> whoever welcomes this child in my name welcomes me, and whoever
> welcomes me welcomes the one who sent me; for the least among all of
> you is the greatest.[1]

Jesus said these amazing words in the context of the disciples arguing between themselves about who was the greatest, and he placed a child in the middle of them.

So, are we equal?

Children, in God's eyes, are very special indeed.

So much so that Jesus, when speaking about children, uses exceptional language as he describes how their angels always look on his Father's face.[2] He does not use language like that about anybody else.

We too need to afford children enormous respect and honour, provide the very best for them, and be ready to learn from them.

We need to "welcome" them, as Jesus says. "Welcome" means to "gladly and cordially receive" or to "invite".

What is our children's experience as they come to our churches?

Are they warmly received in a way that they can appreciate? Jesus adds that if we welcome children, we also welcome him and his Father! What an incredible statement.

Are children shoved out the back, with dirty and inadequate equipment, in uncomfortable spaces with adults who don't really want to be there at all?

Where is Jesus in that?

Principles: what do we really want for our children?

What principles do we have for our children? What do we want them to learn while they are with us in church during these early years?

What do we *really* want?

- To keep them occupied so they don't disturb our worship?
- To give exhausted parents a much-needed break?
- To give them the same sort of experience that we had maybe twenty or thirty years ago ("It didn't do us any harm") so that adults can get on with the serious business of church?
- To train them in the way they should go so that when they are older they will not depart from it?
- To help them have a good knowledge of the Bible?
- To have fun?
- Something else?

Jesus clearly said:

> *"Let the little children come to me; do not stop them; for it is to such as these that the kingdom of God belongs…" And he took them up in his arms, laid his hands on them, and blessed them.*[3]

That needs to be our purpose too.

So how do we let children come to Jesus?

How do we hinder or stop them?

Jesus also rebuked the disciples strongly when they tried to turn mothers with their children away…

We believe that children need to be:

- Safe
- Secure
- Valued
- Respected
- Able to enjoy loving relationships

- Prayed for
- Encouraged to know God, their heavenly Father

What does this actually look like in practice?

When working with three- and four-year-olds in a nursery, I observed a demonstration of valuing a child equally:

> I noticed that when an adult was listening to a child talking, another adult, the headteacher, came up with an "important" message, but the first adult continued to listen to the child until they had finished talking. The adult did this by kneeling to be at the same physical level, gazing into their eyes and being totally "present" to the child. They waited for the child to finish speaking. Then they either finished their conversation or explained to the child that they were going to take that message and be back with them in one minute.
>
> And they were!
>
> In one minute.
>
> In the same way, children were taught that if two adults were talking or another adult and a child, the same framework applied.

This is an example of a "hidden" message which is very powerful. I had to learn how to do this and it took time to get it right, but I felt it was important because of the message it conveyed. It also meant that all children in a group received attention and not just the ones that were the most demanding. It also provided a model to those who did not learn verbally. Being fully "present" to children emotionally, physically and using good body language, says "I value you."

Is that possible in a large group of children?

Yes, it is, on a one-to-one basis.

The other children need to have some degree of independence and security, knowing that their turn will come. From the child's point of view, it is better to have some short, high-quality time with a really important adult, than it is to have no individual attention and always to be treated as part of a group.

This way of "being present" to children is not easy. It can be hard work.

During various aspects of my job I have observed a wide range of strategies that adults employ in order *not* to engage with children (a bit like all the jobs I do around the house in preference to sewing on a button). They do this by talking to other adults, preparing materials, preparing food / drinks, clearing up, cutting out, mixing paints…

Focusing intently on children can reap huge rewards for us as well as them. I have learned so much about individuals from listening closely to them: their joys and interests, their incredible thinking and the way they make connections between one area of life and another. Getting to know and love the children I work with has helped me to recognize how God loves me as his child.

Have you ever been part of a group or crowd and longed that the important speaker / singer / actor / teacher would just have a special private word with you?

It's that search for significance that is in all of us.

Am I important?

Do I belong?

Am I known?

In children's eyes we are like giants. What we do or don't do has an impact on them. We cannot be neutral.

Children and creative thinking

God is the Creator.

The creator of heaven and earth, and everything in it.

Looking at creation – from images of space, to the wonders of life on earth, to the smallest detail of the human body as seen through an electron microscope – the variety and beauty is breath-taking. See Genesis 1 and Job 38 and 39 for God's own list.

All of us at some point must have been filled with awe and wonder.

The elegance of mathematical theory, the way music can touch our souls and the variety of our cultures across the world speak of the joy of a God who thinks outside of the box.

And this Creator God is also our heavenly Father and has made us in his image.

Children in the Way?

We are creative beings.

All of us.

Including children.

From the moment we respond to the sound and smell of our mother, as newborns, we are expressing ourselves. As we grow and develop, we express who we are through speech, what we wear, the things we do and how we relate to others.

Creativity is one of the features that distinguish us from other species. We believe creativity starts within each child as they begin to reach out to explore, with curiosity, the world around. This grows through experimentation or "play". Creativity then draws on imagination and original expression, depending on the feedback of the environment or people. As the child's character develops in response to people, places and things, they can begin to make decisions, take risks and play with ideas.

We believe our children need to be confident to express themselves creatively in order for them to learn with enjoyment. Their creative thinking is about making connections with one area of learning and another as they begin to discover how their world works. Children get feedback from their world through their senses and learn through their active involvement and their interactions with it. This in turn actually influences the wiring of the brain.

Due to new scanning techniques, it has been shown[4] that sensory input actually determines the neuronal (nerve) connections that are made. So, the baby's brain needs early experiences in order to wire the neural circuits of the brain that facilitate learning.[5]

In other words, experience and interactions directly determine the way the brain is wired.

Babies are born with their brains primed for learning.[6]

There is something about the essence of children that they can be creative and expressive and play with materials and ideas. However, unwittingly we can sometimes begin to squash it out of them by giving strong messages about the need to "keep clean" or doing things "the right way".

Whose right way?

I had a new girl, Gemma, start at the nursery with a group of others, and they began to explore the materials available to them. Eventually, after several days she sat down and carefully selected some white paper and coloured pencils. She carefully drew a house and a tree. We were positive in our response to her. The next day she sat down and not only did the same activity but also drew exactly the same picture. I don't mean it was similar, I mean it was almost as accurate as a photocopier. This continued and by the end of the week she had a collection of five identical house drawings which, if you had placed them on top of each other, would have overlapped exactly.

Over time, despite our appreciation of her accurate work, we tried to encourage her to explore other forms of expression by using different media and real objects, but she would refuse, saying she did not know how to draw them. Gemma appeared very frightened of getting it wrong. She had actually been rigidly taught, or rather trained, how to exactly draw the house and the tree and she was scared of attempting anything new that required her to use her own ideas or run the risk of producing something imperfect.

It might be that we, too, have had that creative confidence knocked out of us at some point.

Later we can then unconsciously pass on the same messages to children.

Look at what some of the people from the top of their field say about being creative and pushing boundaries:

Albert Einstein: *"Imagination is more important than knowledge."*

Lord Stone of Blackheath: *"People assume that as an innovator, I break rules. I don't. I relish rules. I just like rewriting them."*[7]

Pablo Picasso: *"All children are artists. The problem [for the child] is how to remain an artist once he grows up."*

Let's look at the wide range of what being creative might mean: painting, drawing, singing, dancing, acting, writing, speaking, running and all sports, cooking, imaginative play, playing an instrument, thinking, playing with mathematical concepts, ideas, dressing, building, sculpting, exploring... the list is endless.

We need to have confidence that the way children express themselves is valuable.

For instance: a while ago when I was teaching three and four year olds, my kind mentor lent me a real lamb, called Joseph, for us to look after for a day! We fed him milk from a bottle and were outside with him all day, along with our usual nursery equipment. We sang, "Baa, baa, black sheep" and "Mary had a little lamb" quite a lot! We took photos to record this wonderful occasion and looked at books with lambs in them.

At the end of the day, I sat down by myself and tried to draw Joseph, and ended up with an incredibly stylized picture which looked a bit like a cloud with four legs sticking out, and I was very disappointed. The next day I provided a range of paper and drawing and painting materials for the children and as we talked over the event, I hoped that we would see lamb pictures. However, little was forthcoming. We made a book together of the photos and of course continued talking.

About two weeks later, there was suddenly a rush of the most beautiful drawings and paintings of Joseph the lamb! They captured the texture of his coat, his movement and essential "lambiness", in a way that I had been unable to do. It was amazing.

It was as if the children needed time to process this new firsthand experience and internalize it in some way, before it came out so expressively in pictorial form.

The children's art was better than mine.

If I had provided outlines of a lamb, drawn by an adult, which in a child's eyes would have carried the hidden message of, "This is how you draw a lamb properly", I don't think the children would have created the same pictures.

If I had given the children pre-drawn lamb pictures, what would the impact have been on them?

Would it have confused their own perceptions and interfered with their reflections?

Having time meant they could process their experiences with the lamb and then draw on their thinking, which eventually came out in their individual creative expressions.

If I had made them sit down and draw a lamb (for mummy/daddy/for the display/for my agenda), the results would also have been different.

In order to release and enable children's creativity we don't need to be confident in our own creative abilities, just willing to support them in their imagination and to be open to God to rediscover our own creativity.

We need to be genuinely respectful of their abilities, provide them with opportunities to express themselves creatively and let them choose when, what and how to do it. And then give feedback about what we genuinely appreciate about their picture (for example).

Becoming a worshipper without inhibitions and with all of our being

> Out in the garden with Evie, then aged thirteen months, I was reminded of what it is to worship. She explored the lawn gingerly, gradually gaining confidence to crawl on her knees, and found the daisies, insects and bird droppings. She was transfixed by them, expressing delight in her new discoveries through giggles and pointing.

How do children worship?

Is it through songs which have no meaning for them?

One of my daughters (aged four) asked: "Why do we sing 'yogurt rains'?" when we sang "Your God reigns" in a marathon singing session.

> As I later played with Evie, I put on a Stevie Wonder CD. Instantly she began to move to the music, giggling and making her own music – her whole being responding to the rhythm.

What is worship?

Why do we worship?

How do we worship – ourselves, you and I?

For me, I worship authentically when I am outside in the natural world, or when I am running, or when I am inspired by some action, music or poetry and am overwhelmed by the greatness of God. I am in relationship with God and am in awe of his magnitude. Yes, I worship corporately with others, but I have learned to do that over the years, and can conform when I have to, but often it is less spontaneous.

Do young children read our hidden messages about worship in church?

What are those messages?

Children are wonderful, intuitive receivers but they are not so good at interpreting the signals they pick up.

Children, designed by a relational Creator, are born to relate. This starts in the womb and is instantly worked on from the moment of birth. They explore the faces of others, searching their eyes to read, "Am I OK? Are you OK?" Their responses are spontaneous – they are great reactors and excellent instigators in forming relationships.

Have you ever stood in a queue in a supermarket behind a very young child who works hard to engage your attention through their eyes, their movements and their language, creating a dance of communication with you? And their relationships are expressed in action – hands raised to be picked up, racing to meet a friend, hugging, punching – all inter-relational actions. In contrast, often when we worship in church we face the front, sing worship songs which are jargon-rich and information-lite and move gently.

What sense do children make of this?

It is my fear that have we sanitized worship so much – made it so cerebral – that we no longer know what it is to "worship God with the whole of our being". In fact, has church become more relevant to our *thinking* than our *relating*? No wonder Jesus said to his friends, "unless you… become like little children"[8] – people who have not lost their spontaneous and responsive delight in their Creator and his creation – people who are not inhibited in their quest to relate to others.

We think that if we worked hard with church members to make churches relevant for children as places where they could express their relationship with God and their relationships with others, they would grow rich in their own identity as members of the community of faith and of the world, and we would actually find we had enriched the worshipping environment for us all.

Is this what Jesus meant by "to become like a little child" when he looked at his competitive friends?

So how do we provide an environment which enables children to experience a creative and loving God?

We need to *hear* them – not just their voices but their communication to us "through the whole of their beings".

As a society, we are very poor listeners. We hear the constant noise of life: iPods, radios, televisions and computer screens all compete for attention, and children's voices get lost in the hubbub.

More insidiously and subconsciously, we listen through the filter of our own experiences of childhood and make assumptions about what children today are saying. But their lives are profoundly different from ours, just as ours are so different from our parents' lives when they were children.

As this book will continue to explore, times are changing, attitudes are changing and research is revealing more and more about the developing child. We need to learn to listen acutely to what children are telling us about their relationship with God and how they express this.

We believe that we are created in the image of God, and that our relationship with him is innate – so do we adults in the church snuff this out over the years with our patronizing attitudes and conformity to traditions that are no longer relevant to this generation?

What do the children in your church appear to really enjoy? How do they worship God?

Reflection

- From a child's viewpoint, what do you think is their experience when they arrive at church?
  - *When they come for the first time?*
  - *When they attend regularly?*
  - *What evidence do you have that they feel warmly welcomed, safe, valued and respected?*
- Spend time watching and observing the children in your church.
  - *What do they really enjoy?*

- – *Do they enjoy being as well as doing?*
- – *How do you know?*
- – *What criteria are you using to make these judgments?*
- Ask yourself: when have I observed a child truly worshipping?
  - – *What were they doing?*
  - – *Where were they?*

CHAPTER 3

Quality Time

I am unique!

Carrie

Made in the image of God

"God *created…*" This is the very first verb in the Bible.

"Through him all things were *made…*" says the third verse of John's Gospel, the New Testament book that starts with "In the beginning…"

A *carpenter…* the trade Jesus learnt from the human father to whom he was given.

Creativity is the first thing mentioned in the Bible and according to the "rule of first mention",[1] this is fundamental to our whole understanding of who God is.

Babies and children are innately creative, expressive and relational beings. There is such joy in supporting children to release their creativity in a wide range of ways. God is the Creator and has made us in his image as creative beings. We may not feel that we are, personally, very creative and there may be many reasons for that (which would make another whole book). Some people have had the creativity squashed out of them.

Where did my creativity go?

We need to think much more broadly about creativity. It is not just a painted picture with an end product that you can hang on a wall. It is about every form of expression that civilization has found: singing, dancing, writing, mark-making of all kinds, cooking, gardening, sculpting, music making, acting, storytelling, expressive language… the list is endless.

We are made in God's image, we are his children and are essentially creative. As creative beings, creativity is the way we explore and interact with our world. It is fundamental to successful learning.

There are around 100 billion stars in our galaxy and 170 billion galaxies in our observable universe. Such knowledge is beyond my comprehension. Just looking at the stars in the night sky speaks so loudly to me.

We have between 10 and 1,000 billion neurones (nerve cells) in our brain. Each of these has between 1,000 and 10,000 connections with other brain cells.

Both of these perspectives – the universe on its grand scale, and an intricate part of our anatomy, on the microscopic scale – fill me at times with awe. I find it hard to keep that perspective; such knowledge is too astonishing for me, and makes me recognize just how competent children are and how great is their capacity to learn. That means I have a deep respect for young children and for their capacity to learn, as demonstrated by their brain development.

As Psalm 139 says, we have been "knit together" amazingly in our mother's womb and we have truly been "fearfully and wonderfully made" (NIV).

We are a dynamic work in progress.

Every day brain connections are made, changed or reinforced.

As babies grow their brains develop many connections and create neural pathways that are directly shaped by the experiences and messages coming through their senses. Early interactions affect the way the brain is wired. Not only do early experiences have a decisive impact on the architecture of the brain in the child, but they go on to influence the nature and extent of adult capabilities.[2]

We can rightly say of brain pathways, *use it or lose it*. A child that has rich sensory experiences in a loving environment will make strong neural pathways that will become more pronounced and give rise to ever-increasing connections and pathways. We know this now because of more recent brain scanning techniques.[3]

If that is true, then is the converse true as well? Yes, sensory deprivation leads to fewer connections being made. Horrendous experiments carried out years ago found that it is not just sensory input that is required, but loving connection and relationship are also essential. Perhaps you remember the images of the Romanian orphanages.

In her book, *The Molecules of Emotion*, Dr Candace Pert,[4] who discovered the first opiate receptor in the brain, convincingly argues that the emotions, mind and body are truly one and cannot be separated from each other in the traditional way. The same neuropeptides that are released, for example, when feelings of well-being are experienced, work in the brain but also have diverse sites all over the body in various organs, including the skin. Similarly, when anxiety levels rise the same is true for those transmitter substances. This has a direct relation to working with babies and young children. How they are feeling will create a background wash of complex chemicals which have a whole-body impact and will affect how they respond to new experiences and new learning.

Therefore new learning cannot take place when anxiety levels are high. This is another reason why our highest priority must be to create a warm, loving and safe environment for our youngest church members.

So: babies are born with their brains primed for learning[5] and are geared to find out how their world works. They learn through using all of their senses and through active participation. Scanning techniques have also shown that when children reach the age of three, their brains are working at a rate twice that of our adult brains!

They have twice the number of our synapses or brain connections, and this continues until they reach the age of ten.

They are learning all of the time! And faster than we adults.

So, where does creativity come in?

What is creativity?

Creativity is fundamental to successful learning, since a child's curiosity and exploration, interacting with their environment and people, help them make connections between one area of learning and another. These connections are literal neural ones, as well as links between ideas and thoughts. As children grow, becoming more confident to experiment, they draw upon previous experiences, use imagination and make decisions, take risks and play with ideas. Creativity helps them to push boundaries in their thinking and extends their world as well as their mental map.

From the youngest baby, to the top scientist, creative thinking is essential.

But this requires time – quality time.

C. G. Jung said: "The creation of something new is not accomplished by the intellect alone but by the play instinct. The creative mind plays with the object it loves."[6]

So, play and being creative are closely linked, and both are essential to learning – even in children's church. Play needs to be understood as a much broader term than the derogatory phrase, "child's play". For example, a good jazz musician plays around the tune competently and creatively, playing with ideas and themes and responding to others spontaneously.

How can we help children to learn through play and being creative?

- By providing them with time to explore and experiment with ideas, materials and activities.
- By helping children feel secure enough to try out new experiences and ways of doing things, as well as being free to rehearse old ones. They need to feel safe enough to take risks, make mistakes and be adventurous in their creative pursuits.
- By valuing children's own ideas rather than expecting them to copy somebody else's.
- By offering children a rich variety of choices, so that they can make decisions about what they do, and the chance to get engrossed in what interests them.
- By making sure young children have the support of sensitive and responsive adults working alongside them.

When children are being creative they exhibit some of these features:

- A sense of curiosity and wonder
- Openness to new experiences
- A capacity to take risks
- Breaking boundaries or thinking outside the box
- Expressing their unique views and ideas
- Developing imaginatively
- Self-expression
- Utilizing their senses

The process of creativity

It is the process of creativity that is its most important aspect. This is because when there are high levels of concentration, the cognitive processes are complex and many different areas of the brain are being used, and many connections are being made. The end products, which adults tend to focus on, often do not reflect their input. Adults who are important to the child need to understand and respect that journey and give genuine praise for the effort that has been contributed.

If there is to be an end product, it needs to be decided by the child.

A good example of this happened after I took my nursery class to Bristol Zoo. On return to the nursery, Saskia went over to the art table and selected a large sheet of paper and chose her paints carefully. As she began to paint she showed deep levels of concentration: her breathing slowed, she moved her brush with precision and she narrated her painting in a low voice to herself. I caught snatches of it: "... the flamingo... pink... long neck... standing on one leg... black beak... then it rained... and rained... there!" "There" was pronounced with great satisfaction. Her painting was deliberate, detailed and expressive and contained all the elements she talked about. When she reached the bit about the rain, she picked up the black brush and painted the rain with great sweeps covering the whole picture. The end result was a black sheet of paper!

However, Saskia's concentration and satisfaction with her work demonstrated to me that she had expressed herself in a way that she was pleased with and had recounted an important experience. In my opinion, creativity had been expressed and important learning had taken place; judging the end product alone would have done Saskia a disservice. Therefore it is important to place a high value on children's individual expressions and the work and effort that have gone into the process.

Am I learning what you are teaching?

From the child's point of view, are they learning what you think they are learning?

Learning is a complex process. Just as the wiring of the brain is complex and non-linear, so is learning. Learning can be messy, uneven and intricate. It very rarely happens in a straight line. Even very young children can concentrate on an activity for long periods of time, if they are motivated by it.

> I once observed a boy of eight months play with the pages and contents of a book for twenty-five minutes with an interested adult who sensitively followed his lead. The adult listened closely to the child and gave gentle support with page-turning before the child became frustrated by their lack of dexterity. At times the adult talked about the picture and pointed; at other times the child pointed and "talked" while the adult listened.

How did this happen and can we make it happen again?

I believe this happened because the child, not the adult, chose the activity from a selection of resources at hand. They were motivated and were able to concentrate because they were content – warm, fed, rested, feeling secure and happy. At another time the same child might be much more interested in developing a relationship or eating or manipulating various objects or any number of other activities. We need to respect the young child, realizing that they are learning all the time, and we need to support whatever direction they choose during the short time we have them at church. So the answer to the question above is that no, we cannot *make* it happen again, but we can *offer* it as one option.

Are children learning what I am teaching?

A common mistake is that adults feel they are "teaching" when they are speaking to a child (which is a legacy from the "empty vessel" theory, that a child is like an empty glass into which the teacher pours knowledge). Adults spend a lot of time speaking to even young children in a monologue. Very little of that will be remembered.

What will be remembered is what the child interacted with using all of their senses, what they chose to become involved in, what they were thinking and what other feelings they were experiencing at that time.

However, if a true dialogue takes place, with the adult following the child's lead, listening closely, then a learning journey can begin to take place.

Therefore we need to reappraise what our teaching aims are for children of various ages, bearing in mind their developmental needs. We need to recognize that children are learning all of the time. If there is a big mismatch between their needs, and the expectations of the powerful adults around them at church, they will be thinking: "I don't like it here... I don't belong... I am not good enough... I am anxious... I am bored." Later on, heading towards the teenage years, they may in effect become fully inoculated, and when they can vote with their feet, they will leave church.

Is this an unreasonable assumption?

Not from my experience of talking to disaffected children of church families.

How can we help our young children learn to learn?

Really what we are asking is: What learning attitudes and dispositions do we want children to have?

There are many lists, but here is one that I have found it helpful to ponder:

- Confidence
- Independence
- Curiosity
- A high level of involvement
- Self-motivation
- Persistence
- Risk taking
- Concentration
- Sense of self

These attitudes and dispositions are learnt when children are young, and they then become the way they approach the world. Indeed, I have taught children who, at the age of seven, have already learnt that they cannot "do" formal learning and have switched off from the education system. It is very hard, but not impossible, to reconnect them.

Professor Sir Harold Kroto, a Nobel Prize-winning chemist, said: "Nine out of ten of my experiments fail, and that is considered a pretty good record amongst scientists."[7]

Our children do indeed need to learn the persistence and resilience expressed here. They also need to learn that it is OK to fail. They need a sense of self-belief and self-confidence in order to persevere in their learning.

Henry Ford, the automobile magnate, said: "Whether you think you can or whether you think you can't, you are probably right."

Bearing all this in mind, then, how do we teach children about God, the Bible and where they are in God's family?

This is where the book is heading, and we will give clear guidelines, but it is of vital importance that the foundations that we are covering here are understood and applied. They are the framework and context into which we can put our ideas for the spiritual content that has overriding importance, and this cannot be compromised or glossed over. We cannot overstate how invaluable it is to spend time understanding the basics about child development, how children learn, the atmosphere we need to create and the attitude we need to have.

Moving times

One of the main ways church children are set up to fail is that they are expected to sit still for too long. Sadly, many children, notably boys, get the "naughty" label for behaving boisterously.

Is this because they are not brought up strictly enough? After all, the Victorians expected little children to be seen and not heard, and children had to do as they were told. Is it just because of our *laisser-faire* attitude that we have "lower" standards? This is an interesting debate. Some current research into children's muscular development will throw light on our thinking.

Sally Goddard Blythe, Director of the Institute of Neuro-Physiological Psychology, has carried out extensive research and written several books,[8] and her thinking underpins much of what we want to say here.[9]

When babies are born they have certain reflexes to touch that make them respond physically: stroking a baby's cheek causes her or him to turn towards that touch and search for a nipple or teat to feed from – the "rooting reflex". This then helps them to develop visual recognition of the caregiver, and then sight and visual recognition take over from the touch reflex.

By about six months this reflex action becomes suppressed by the higher brain levels. What starts as the conscious control of balance, posture and coordination, gradually becomes "postural reflexes" which are unconscious. As these become unconscious and the child learns to walk, so the control of these functions shifts from the outer cortex of the brain to lower brain levels. This then frees up the higher levels of the brain for higher thinking such as understanding all the sensory input, analysing it, relational dialogue, logical thinking and processing. If a baby or young child is given many opportunities to develop physically – controlling their muscles for large and small movements, for balance and coordination – then this happens naturally in its own time. However, if not enough experiences are given, then a young child's outer cortex will still be taken up with postural coordination and will have less room for higher thinking skills, thus affecting their development.

Young babies need to spend most of their time on the floor, with gentle rough-and-tumble play or being held or carried rather than kept in confined spaces such as static baby chairs. This is because they are gathering valuable sensory information that continuously stimulates the balance mechanism. When they are being carried or rocked, this is calming because their sensory system responds to movement, and is reminiscent of their time in the womb.

Continuous touch helps the babies to develop their body map.

Lying on the floor on their tummies or back and moving their limbs, babies are "learning" about where they are in space and how their limbs work. Babies who have been deprived of these sensory experiences often later have difficulties not just with physical competency but also with language development.

This is relevant to church, which therefore needs to provide appropriate surfaces for babies to lie down on, and enough interested adults to hold or carry them when needed.

Learning how to sit is a complex series of skills, and babies need lots of practice. Babies should not be given too much help, such as a rigid seat which would hold them in a sitting position without them using many muscles, because they need to develop the reflexes so that when they lose balance, the hand comes out to break the fall. This is called the "parachute reflex" and is an essential reflex for being able to sit, as well as for standing later on.

So the church needs to provide surfaces, cushions and adults who will help the baby along the way but not do too much. A helpful term is "scaffolding", where the adult provides a helpful structure that allows the baby to grow in competence and safety so that when the scaffolding is removed, the child's ability is sound.

As children reach the age of around three years they seem to be expected to sit for long periods of time, especially during a morning in church.

This is one of the main ways children are set up to fail. Their muscle development is still at an early stage, with boys developing at a slower rate than girls. Sally Goddard Blythe says the hardest and most "advanced form of movement is the ability to sit totally still, requiring whole muscle groups to work together".[10] Just as it is easier to balance on a two-wheeler bike when it is moving, so it is easier for a child to be in balance while they are moving, rather than when they are static.

Therefore in the age group from three to seven there are likely to be many children, with more boys than girls, who are physically not mature enough to sit still.

They cannot do it. Their brains and muscles have not yet developed that ability.

They are not naughty or disruptive.

And yet many of our young children in church receive negative messages about themselves – in the place where God is worshipped, the One who made children to develop in that way. In the very place where they should feel safe, they are receiving disapproval, and are expected to perform a physical task that they are incapable of. We need to structure our programme so they are not expected to sit for long at all.

In fact, the way to help them develop greater muscle control is to give them more physical exercise!

We need to adapt to their needs, not the other way round. Therefore limiting the time they are expected to sit is acknowledging their essential requirements, and giving them activities where they can move around is more likely to engage their interests. It is also more likely that they will be learning what they are involved in instead of learning: "I am uncomfortable… my legs hurt… I'm getting told off again."

Remember that learning is non-linear, and so a child might be more able to sit for longer at certain times than others, and motivation affects that too.

How can we help children?

We need to provide opportunities for them to be active, to use their muscles and enjoy interesting experiences. We need to plan a session that does not require them to sit for so long.

For example: I had a young group of mostly three year olds and knew that sitting for a short story was not appropriate for some of them. The story that week was Jesus calming the storm at sea. I asked around and found that somebody could lend me a small inflatable dinghy for the morning! So as the session started, we all discussed the "boat" in the room and their experiences of boats as they had their juice and fruit. Then, having eaten, we all got in the boat as I told the story from memory (in a very short form). The children all joined in to actively create the feeling of being tossed by the waves by rocking the dinghy to and fro, imitating the howling wind, commanding "Peace, be still" all together, and then the sudden calm. This was repeated several times while the interest was there. Then they went and chose other activities but came back to re-enact the scene using the boat themselves whenever they wanted to.

It took time, energy and creative thinking to make that resource available for the children, but it was so worthwhile. It is amazing the resources that are available through church and friends.

Many churches have limited space but creative opportunities are still possible.

One resource that is often neglected that some churches actually do have is outside space.

Remember a happy time in your childhood. Where were you?

If you ask a group of adults to reflect on a happy occasion in their childhood, around 80 per cent of them will recall an event taking place outside. When asked what they were enjoying, a wide range of experiences are often described. However, common themes are: making dens/houses; making mud pies/rose-petal perfume; imaginary adventures; playing in the street; off all day over the fields; climbing trees; riding bikes; exploring and having adventures and playing with other children with no adults around.

In fact one of the pioneers of early education, Margaret McMillan, many years ago declared: "The best classroom and the richest cupboard is roofed only by the sky" – which I fully agree with.

Colleagues working in Denmark have children from birth to six years spending many hours outside through all weathers (many degrees below freezing, as their climate is harsher than Britain's), because they believe that it is healthier and a better learning environment for children. They say, "There is no such thing as bad weather, only bad clothing."

They also think we are cruel to sit four year olds down and force them to write when their hands are not fully developed. I, once again, concur!

Many children are far happier outside, and nurseries that have changed their practice to include more outside play have discovered that the amount of conflict between children is radically reduced.

Do your church children have frequent conflicts? Try taking them outside for part of the session… or all of the session!

Why are we reluctant to take children outside?

Tina Bruce highlights one reason when she says: "There is a bizarre assumption that knowledge gained inside is superior to that gained outside."[11]

All learning is learning, wherever it takes place. Helping children to spend some time outside during church can transform their experiences into positive ones. It is great to have space to move freely, to run around, to be able to make mess without worry, to explore all that nature offers, even on tarmac and, of course, in the great British weather!

It's true – bad weather looks worse through a window!

It can be exciting being outside in the rain and wind, and their energy is somehow invigorating. Snow can be exhilarating and sometimes magical in its transformation of our environment. And there is nothing like that feeling of coming in from a shared experience of a blustery day outside into the warmth of a familiar room with a new sense of companionship.

Quite often the biggest obstacle to going outside is the adults themselves.

When I started work in a nursery not too long ago, in preparation I treated myself to a warm pair of gloves, a hat and a scarf, as I feel the cold badly. So even though I had to spend large periods of the day outside, I was comfortable and able to follow the children's interests there, which even included reading stories in below-freezing temperatures, because that was where they wanted to be read to.

Outside is a place where emotions can be expressed loudly, and the wonderful feeling of endorphins (natural opiates) being released after physical exercise gives a sense of great well-being. I have also found that carrying a distressed child outside for a wander can have a calming effect.

Some churches do not even have part of a car park that can be made safe for children. However, it is still worthwhile to organize a trip to the park or a friend's garden as a special event, because of the positive shared experience together as a group.

Psalm 139 reminds us of how intimately God is involved with forming us, from our conception onwards. As human babies we are born in a fairly under-developed state – unlike, for example, an antelope calf, which can run within hours of being born. So God entrusts us with the care and nurture of babies as they grow. As churches too, we have the responsibility to lovingly provide the very best quality time for our most precious members.

Reflection

- How can you celebrate the uniqueness of each child in your church group?
  - *Add up the amount of time a three year old spends sitting down throughout a church morning. Add another fifteen minutes if they arrive by car.*
  - *Thinking creatively, is there any way you can reduce this length of time by providing engaging activity for them?*
- Close your eyes and think back to a time in your early childhood when you were enjoying yourself outside.
  - *Where were you?*
  - *Who were you with?*
  - *Were you alone?*
  - *What was happening?*
  - *What could you smell? (The olfactory centre of the brain is next to the long-term memory centre.)*
  - *What were you experiencing?*
  - *What were you learning?*
  - *How can you recreate some of those experiences and opportunities for your children in church?*

The Little Boy

Once a little boy went to school.
He was quite a little boy
And it was quite a big school.
But when the little boy
Found that he could go to his room
By walking right in from the door outside
He was happy;
And the school did not seem
Quite so big anymore.

One morning
When the little boy had been in school awhile,
The teacher said:
"Today we are going to make a picture."
"Good!" thought the little boy.
He liked to make all kinds;
Lions and tigers,
Chickens and cows,
Trains and boats;
And he took out his box of crayons
And began to draw.

But the teacher said, "Wait!"
"It is not time to begin!"
And she waited until everyone looked ready.
"Now," said the teacher,
"We are going to make flowers."
"Good!" thought the little boy,
He liked to make beautiful ones
With his pink and orange and blue crayons.
But the teacher said "Wait!"
"And I will show you how."
And it was red, with a green stem.
"There," said the teacher,
"Now you may begin."

The little boy looked at his teacher's flower
Then he looked at his own flower.
He liked his flower better than the teacher's
But he did not say this.
He just turned his paper over,
And made a flower like the teacher's.
It was red, with a green stem.

On another day
When the little boy had opened
The door from the outside all by himself,
The teacher said:
"Today we are going to make something with clay."
"Good!" thought the little boy;
He liked clay.
He could make all kinds of things with clay:
Snakes and snowmen,
Elephants and mice,

Cars and trucks
And he began to pull and pinch
His ball of clay.

But the teacher said, "Wait!"
"It is not time to begin!"
And she waited until everyone looked ready.
"Now," said the teacher,
"We are going to make a dish."
"Good!" thought the little boy,
He liked to make dishes.
And he began to make some
That were all shapes and sizes.

But the teacher said "Wait!"
"And I will show you how."
And she showed everyone how to make
One deep dish.
"There," said the teacher,
"Now you may begin."

The little boy looked at the teacher's dish;
Then he looked at his own.
He liked his better than the teacher's
But he did not say this.
He just rolled his clay into a big ball again
And made a dish like the teacher's.
It was a deep dish.

And pretty soon
The little boy learned to wait,
And to watch
And to make things just like the teacher.
And pretty soon
He didn't make things of his own anymore.

Then it happened
That the little boy and his family

Moved to another house,
In another city,
And the little boy
Had to go to another school.
This school was even bigger
Than the other one.
And there was no door from the outside
Into his room.
He had to go up some big steps
And walk down a long hall
To get to his room.
And the very first day
He was there,
The teacher said:
"Today we are going to make a picture."
"Good!" thought the little boy.
And he waited for the teacher
To tell what to do.
But the teacher didn't say anything.
She just walked around the room.

When she came to the little boy
She asked, "Don't you want to make a picture?"
"Yes," said the little boy.
"What are we going to make?"
"I don't know until you make it," said the teacher.
"How shall I make it?" asked the little boy.
"Why, anyway you like," said the teacher.
"And any colour?" asked the little boy.
"Any colour," said the teacher.
"If everyone made the same picture,
And used the same colours,
How would I know who made what,
And which was which?"
"I don't know," said the little boy.
And he began to make a red flower with a green stem.

Helen Buckley[1]

Section 2

So Last Sunday!

So where are we going wrong? Perhaps we are caught up in the last century in terms of our engagement with children in church, even though we live in the present one and are working hard to "do church for the twenty-first century" for adults and adolescents.

This section will raise some of the questions, consider some of the current research and discuss some strategies drawing on current work with young children in society.

CHAPTER 4

Past Times

Have children changed?

Isobel

I guess the answer to this question is yes and no! Certainly, attitudes towards young children have changed, society has changed and the world has grown smaller; but our basic human needs remain the same. Maslow, a well-known psychologist, devised a pyramid of needs, starting with the basic needs for survival including food, water and shelter, then working up through needs for love and affection, to the ultimate goal of self-actualization.[1] This theory is true for all people of all ages, and care services in the UK are based on this.[2]

Children, then, have not essentially changed in terms of their basic needs.

Physically children *do* seem to be changing. They are more prone to obesity, puberty starts earlier and children are taller than previous generations; but are these evolutionary changes, or based on our changing lifestyle?

Historically, we have tended to view children through developmental knowledge and understanding located within the tradition of science and later, psychology. Children were measured by "norms".

I have non-identical twin daughters and I remember that when they started school, the school doctor examined them, as was the routine practice in the 1980s. One daughter was on the "correct" percentile but the other dropped well below it. We were called back for repeated visits to check her progress, although it felt as if it was me that was being checked out. As I lay awake one night worrying that the doctor thought I was neglecting one of my children, it occurred to me that I am petite, and so is my mother. On our next visit I said to the doctor, "Look at me. I'm not very big and neither is my mother."

We were never given another appointment, and years later, when my daughter, then a teenager, had her school medical, the doctor looked at her as she entered the room and said, "Did you have a problem with your weight? I notice that you were weighed frequently when you were young." She was average height and perfectly normal.

Developmental norms were how children were measured and judged in all aspects of their development, correlating with their age. The danger of this is that we lose sight of the individual child. If a child is concentrating on becoming a skilled walker, they may not be concentrating so much on becoming a proficient talker. Although children pass through the same stages, they do so at different rates depending on their genes, environment, experiences, health and interests.

So is there another way that we can examine and understand children and childhood?

Sociology became a very popular science in the 1960s and it introduced the notion of *social construction* into studies of children. Social construction is the way that people within a society give meaning to particular social concepts, activities and situations, based on their own society and culture. It is the way that we, as a society, construct our views and beliefs about life and all that it consists of.

Gender is a good example of this.

Debates on what it means to be female vary around the world and across cultures, beliefs and traditions, dependent on these variations.

Childhood can also be seen to be a social construction with global variations on what is considered to be a child and how childhood is perceived within a given society.

The idea of social construction gave rise to *social constructivism*, a term from psychology which refers to the way in which individual children (or adults) construct their knowledge, based on their interactions with others within the context of their environment, their culture and the society in which they live. Social constructivism is concerned with how individual children construct their own lives. In current practice, we are aware of the "agency" of children – their ability to influence the decisions made with them or about them. You may know of the term "social actors" – children are co-players with adults on the stage of life.

Both social construction and social constructivism are fluid concepts, changing with time and place.

If we accept this notion of social construction, it is no surprise that attitudes towards childhood and children have changed throughout history.

According to Philippe Aries, a French historian writing in the twentieth century, childhood as a separate category is a modern phenomenon. He suggests that although in medieval times children were not treated differently from adults or seen as a distinct group, this did not mean that they were neglected or badly treated. They were seen as mini-adults, wearing the same clothes and sharing in many of the same activities, as illustrated in classical paintings and portraits. He then continues to explore the changing attitudes towards and views of children through the centuries. However, many of Aries' hypotheses were based on art in history, and of course the subjects for artists were often commissioned by wealthy patrons, who were men, and not necessarily typical of the average family or society – nor were they the perception of women and mothers!

Neil Postman, an English sociologist, claims that the invention of childhood was due to the development of technology – not the internet, but the printing press around 1450! As a result of the greater ease for producing books, no longer requiring a dedicated monk to handwrite with a quill and ink, adults became aware of the importance of learning for children and so children began to emerge as a significant group in society.

Religion has always played an important role in the way that children are perceived. Christianity was the religion in England from Saxon times, whether it was Protestant or Catholic. Children were thought to be born in sin and therefore naturally sinful. The notion of original sin probably originated from a biblical interpretation of the sin of Adam and Eve in Genesis 3. It was St Augustine who stated that original sin was inherited sin (based on Psalm 51:5) and other theologians agreed with him. The role of parents and other adults was to save children from this through beatings for "bad" behaviour, learning the catechism by heart and learning to read the Bible. This was the primary purpose of learning to read – to become good.

This resulted in a punitive attitude towards children and is commonly termed "the Puritan discourse" of childhood.

Due to poor sanitation and health, many infants did not survive in childhood and so baptism of young children was very important to ensure that their souls would be received into heaven.

During the seventeenth century, attitudes towards children began to change with the introduction of toys, books and artefacts. John Locke, a prominent philosopher, proposed the notion that the child was born as a blank slate (a *tabula rasa*). He rejected the idea that children are naturally wicked. He suggested that children are born neutral and it is the role of the adults around them to help them to "write their own lives" through appropriate experiences and opportunities. It was considered that it was the responsibility of adults to teach them and discipline them so they would grow up to become good, upright citizens. This required strict discipline and the "moulding" of the child – which was, of course, based on an adult perspective of what a good person should be and who the child should become.

Are any of these views of the child present in our thinking about children in our churches today?

Are they biblical?

What does God think about childhood?

How would we know?

As the middle class developed, young children were protected economically and formal education was more important for boys; women and girls only needed to know how to raise a family and care for the home!

For the majority of children growing up within the working class, children worked to contribute to the family income, and this also kept them occupied and out of trouble. In towns their work might well be industrial; in rural communities children would undertake agricultural work, or work at the family home. The type of work carried out by each child was dependent on age, geography, work opportunities and gender.

During the period of the Enlightenment, in the eighteenth century, Jean-Jacques Rousseau, a Swiss philosopher and influential thinker, introduced the idea of a child-centred view of childhood. In his book *Emile* he proposed that children are born innocent and are corrupted by society, and that society could be changed through an appropriate education of children. Rousseau suggested that adults should observe the child's interests, then use this information to develop what the child needs to learn, rather than assuming what the child should know. He also inferred that children need to be protected from all that might corrupt them.

During the period of industrialization, there were concerns about children working in dangerous situations, about education, health, homelessness and child poverty. Great pioneers for children such as Dr Barnardo and George Muller set up children's homes for orphans, and organizations such as The Salvation Army worked hard to support the poor and homeless.

By the end of the Victorian era there was a recognized need for the intervention of the state to address the appalling conditions that so many people in England lived in.

Concerns about the health of the soldiers fighting in the Boer War led the government to reflect on the health care of young children. How could malnourished children grow up to have the energy and strength to defend Britain? So to put it simplistically, the welfare state was conceived and became firmly established throughout the twentieth century.

As that century progressed, interest in childhood increased and became centre stage for a variety of reasons.

Children's Rights were first mooted by Eglantyne Jebb following the First World War. She and her sister, Geraldine Buxton, worked with the impoverished children in Europe who were victims of the war. The two sisters recognized that though children were entitled to Human Rights, they also needed their own set of specific rights to protect their specific needs. Although it took a further sixty-seven years to ratify these rights internationally, organizations working with children now are required to respect their rights and work in participation with children, acknowledging their rights to be involved in decisions that are made about them, and their place as social actors.

Children's Rights fall into four categories:

- Prevention of harm
- Protection from harm
- Provision of basic needs including health, education and well-being
- Participation, so that children are included and involved in decisions made about them

We can see, then, how history, circumstances, politics and economics have each impacted on the view that society holds of children at any given time. Throughout the Victorian era, we might consider that the Puritan discourse of childhood was predominant, with its punitive view of discipline, and its children's rhymes and literature, which included breathtaking cautionary tales!

Children's experiences were very much divided by class and economic experience, but nevertheless, strict discipline, moral conduct and "good" manners prevailed.

Children in the Way?

In more recent years our view of children has become more blurred. Do we have the right to say what is right or wrong?

At times it seems that we can be overwhelmed with a Romantic discourse of childhood, particularly related to young babies. Images of innocence are depicted in advertisements of naked babies or children dressed in white or pastel colours. Conversely, we revert to the Puritan discourse when we read about "hoodies" and "feral" children running wild in our streets.

In our "blame" culture, do we blame the children? Or the parents? Or society?

> As Evie (aged two years three months) and I were out in Borough High Street, she in her "hoodie" and helmet speeding along on her scooter, weaving in and out of people and imitating the body movements she must have observed from skateboarders, and me in quick pursuit with Niall in the buggy, I chuckled to myself that "hoodie" vandals are getting younger and younger!

We are inundated by advice on how to bring up children. Programmes on television and radio broadcast horror stories of families who are struggling with challenging children, while a plethora of experts provide their different strategies for survival. At the time of writing, the themes of food, property and challenging children seem to dominate the airwaves.

Why?

What has happened?

What has changed?

A useful activity for church, youth and children's leaders is to look at advertisements, news coverage, films, documentaries and newspapers, and consider the image of the child that is portrayed in our society. Are children a gift, a commodity, a chance for adults to relive their own childhoods or to find success through them?

What is a child? When does childhood begin? When does it end? How would we know? Under British legislation, a child can get married at sixteen, but not vote until they are eighteen. They can fight for their country in wars at sixteen but not drive a car until they are seventeen. Children in England start school in the year they are five years old and can leave when they are eighteen. They are deemed by law to be criminally responsible at the age of ten.

No wonder we are confused!

So what about the children? Do they become corrupted by society or are they born bad?

What do children say?

In 2007 UNICEF produced a report on children's well-being in the twenty-one most developed countries – notably the richest countries in the world. To our shame, Britain came bottom of the table, with the United States of America a close second from the bottom. This report was the result of researching the views of children within the wealthy countries. The report suggested that families in Britain are less cohesive and that there are greater inequalities within UK society.

In his response to the UNICEF report, Richard Layard suggests that the common theme throughout the findings by UNICEF is the "excessive individualism" found in contemporary British society.

In 2008, the Children's Society carried out a research project into the lives of children in the UK aged eleven to sixteen years. Richard Layard and Judy Dunn responded to these findings and proposed that in order to flourish, children need:

- Loving families
- Friends
- A positive lifestyle
- Solid values
- Good schools
- Positive mental health
- Enough money

These can be explored further in their book, *A Good Childhood*,[3] but it is important for church leaders to be aware of what children are saying in our contemporary society.

What are children interested in?

How can we facilitate their knowledge and understanding of God through these interests?

We will explore this theme in the later chapters.

In a significant development, the most recent curriculum for young children in England, *The Early Years Foundation Stage* (EYFS, 2007), notes that identifying and supporting children's interests is both encouraged and directed. While there are controversial aspects to this curriculum, there tends to be common agreement that the principles upon which it is based are sound and appropriate. I agree, and I consider that they are echoed in the Bible. There are four themes, each supported by a key principle:

- A unique child. Every child is a competent learner from birth who can be resilient, capable, confident and self-assured.

- Positive relationships. Children learn to be strong and independent from a base of loving and secure relationships with parents and/or a key person.

- Enabling environments. The environment plays a key role in supporting and extending children's development and learning.

- Learning and development. Children develop and learn in different ways and at different rates, and all areas of learning and development are equally important and interconnected.

The Early Years Foundation Stage is a play-based curriculum which not only values play but also acknowledges that young children learn through it. Although there are still some people who advocate that children should start formal education at the age of four, most experts within early years agree with the Cambridge Review[4] that formal education should start at six years, in line with many other European countries such as Sweden and Denmark.

Why?

Could it be that research about the developing brain, studies on how young children learn and the importance of children becoming confident communicators and social actors are now more widely recognized? Could it be that we are increasingly realizing that play is children's *work*, and that children really do learn through meaningful and purposeful play. "Meaningful" and "purposeful" do not mean that the play is adult-led and highly structured, but that it makes sense to the child and is of importance to her or him; this does not just mean occupying or entertaining the children.

In a global world we are influenced by international approaches to children's education, cultural diversity in ways of nurturing them as well as concerns about their health and well-being. In recent years research has been a large factor in our growing awareness of the needs of children in the twenty-first century. Unsurprisingly, the current trends are taking us back to the thinking and innovation of past pioneers for children's education.

So where does this leave us in our programmes for children in *church*? What do we make of the principles of the Early Years Foundation Stage?

What are the principles which underpin *our* work with children?

Have children changed or is it our understanding of them that has changed?

If we could sit still for hours when we were young, why can't children now?

So how do we respond to this thinking in the church? Are we stuck in the Puritan discourse, trying to make our children good; or in the *tabula rasa* concept, trying to write what we think is right on children's lives; or do we value the uniqueness of each child?

If we reflect on Psalm 139:1–18,[5] what does David the psalmist suggest?

> *O Lord, you have searched me and known me.*
> *You know when I sit down and when I rise up;*
> *you discern my thoughts from far away.*
> *You search out my path and my lying down,*
> *and are acquainted with all my ways.*
> *Even before a word is on my tongue,*
> *O Lord, you know it completely.*
> *You hem me in, behind and before,*
> *and lay your hand upon me.*
> *Such knowledge is too wonderful for me;*
> *it is so high that I cannot attain it.*
> *Where can I go from your spirit?*
> *Or where can I flee from your presence?*
> *If I ascend to heaven, you are there;*
> *if I make my bed in Sheol, you are there.*
> *If I take the wings of the morning*
> *and settle at the farthest limits of the sea,*
> *even there your hand shall lead me,*
> *and your right hand shall hold me fast.*
> *If I say, "Surely the darkness shall cover me,*

and the light around me become night,"
even the darkness is not dark to you;
the night is as bright as the day,
for darkness is as light to you.
For it was you who formed my inward parts;
you knit me together in my mother's womb.
I praise you, for I am fearfully and wonderfully made.
Wonderful are your works;
that I know very well.
My frame was not hidden from you,
when I was being made in secret,
intricately woven in the depths of the earth.
Your eyes beheld my unformed substance.
In your book were written
all the days that were formed for me,
when none of them as yet existed.
How weighty to me are your thoughts, O God!
How vast is the sum of them!
I try to count them – they are more than the sand;
I come to the end – I am still with you.

I can't remember how I occupied myself in church before the age of five. We lived in Nigeria and church services were very long but very lively. My 91-year-old mother has told me that I was bored! The services were in Hausa, the local language, and after the first hymn or so, she would take us four children home. Very few women and children attended church for this reason. We all went to Sunday School in the afternoon, again in Hausa. I have no recollection of these experiences. I have many memories of growing up in Nigeria and my experiences have had a huge influence on me and my life through the years. So is it significant that I have buried the memories of church and Sunday School?

As a five year old, back in England, sitting next to my grandmother in church, I remember her feeding me with her disgusting cough sweets to keep me quiet. I noted the distinctive mannerisms of certain adults, keeping a tally of them in my head and looking out for them each week. Later, at the age of ten, my sister and I would listen for the slightest murmur from our baby sister, as this meant we could go out to look after her.

I was an imaginative, physical child who found sitting still very hard – and now I know there are scientific reasons for this, which suggest that I was normal, not naughty!

Coincidentally, now I work in one of the ex-Muller homes in Bristol, which is now a college of further education. The University Centre is on the top floor overlooking the city and the Gloucestershire County Cricket ground. There are long corridors and the windows in the rooms are too high to look out of – all you can see is sky-scapes, which, stunning as they can be, would not have helped the children to connect with the social world around them. This was considered to be appropriate for children growing up in Victorian Britain – no distractions for them! In today's Western society, we would not dream of designing buildings for young children like this. Nor would we countenance the idea of children sleeping in large dormitories in institutional buildings that can accommodate 2,000 children.

Why?

Our thinking has changed as we co-construct society for the current generation. How has this influenced what we do with our youngest children in church?

Are we still reliant on pre-prepared materials and adult-led activities with an adult concept of a theme? Is it Trinity Sunday next week? How can we teach the children about the Trinity? What does the book suggest?

Most of us have grown up through a period of increasing wealth and are part of a consumer, throw-away, take-away society. We are increasingly aware of inequalities in the UK, the growing gap between poverty and wealth. Faced with a global financial crisis, with our country in debt and close to bankruptcy, we are faced with the consequences of our own greed as a stark reality. Times are changing and our lifestyles will have to change. Children will be affected by our changing attitudes. We have the opportunity as Christians to have a long think about the degree to which consumerism and individualism have seeped into our churches.

Do we want this for our children? If not, we need to reflect, pray and act to change our own ways. We cannot take others where are not willing to go ourselves.

Today there are other issues that face us in today's society: the high status that is given to academic education and qualifications, at the cost of skilled trades; family structures are changing and evolving, and the traditional nuclear family cannot be assumed for all children. Families may be mobile and communities may change their demographic make-up as we become more multicultural. The world is not such a big place because travel, technology and communication link people in a closer relationship than ever before. Social networking has become an established way of keeping in touch and information is "out there" for everyone. We can see the world in action from the comfort of our settee, in the safety of our own homes – but are we desensitized by the huge volume of information that overwhelms us, without being able to do anything about it? Our very youngest children are also affected by all this. This is the world that they live in and know. They are not immune.

I am not saying that all this change and the speed of change in our lifetime is bad. Far from it. But we do need to acknowledge today's faster pace of life and the impact that all these changes make upon us and upon our churches.

Has technology only enabled us to put on fantastic presentations, which do not require the participation of the people in the congregation, or are children aware of relationships – something they crave – as being most important? Do we adults expect to be "done to" or to be "involved in"?

It is acknowledged within education that parents are the first and foremost educators of their children. *They* will be the strongest influence on their children's developing sense of attitudes, values and beliefs.

But, "It takes a village to raise a child." This well-known statement is a reality. We are not just a collection of isolated individuals, and this is particularly true for members of a church. Bronfenbrenner[6] proposed the Ecological Systems Theory, situating the child in a nest of contexts, rather like Russian dolls – each layer impacting on the child at the centre. However, Bronfenbrenner goes on to suggest that the child too has an impact on each of the contexts.

This theory reinforces the view that children are active agents who influence the world around them, but it is also an important theory for church leaders to consider. Everything that happens within the church will impact on the youngest as well as the oldest member of that church community.

Sometimes we need to ask other members of the church for support. I remember having a large, lively group of children including several energetic boys. I felt that one boy in particular would benefit from additional attention from a man, and that I was not the best person to support him.

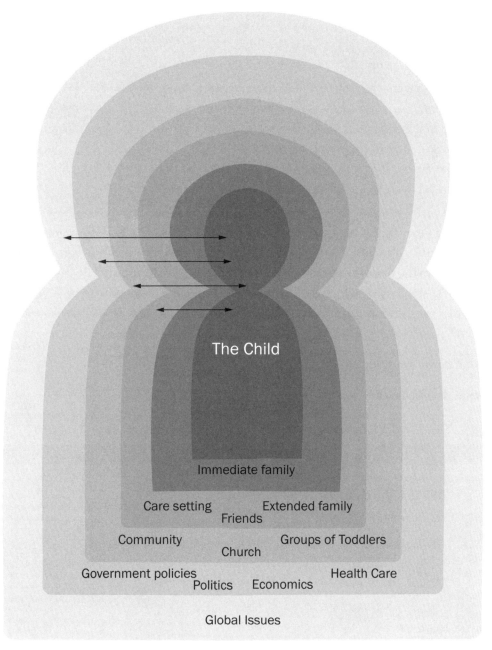

The Child

Immediate family

Care setting   Extended family
        Friends

Community   Groups of Toddlers
        Church

Government policies   Health Care
        Politics   Economics

Global Issues

"Nesting Dolls" – directional influences
based on Bronfenbrenner's theory

My husband discovered that they shared an interest in aeroplanes, so he invited this child to come and build a model plane with him. Each week they met in our house. I would provide the refreshments and they would work hard on their model making. This time with my husband showed him that we were genuinely interested in him. His opinions were important and his skills were valued. This affirmation seemed to increase his confidence and help him to feel at ease with us. As a consequence, his behaviour in the group changed too. Within a few weeks I noticed that this child and I had formed a better relationship together. He joined in with activities and appeared to enjoy the group. I think he knew that I both respected and valued him.

Over the years, times have changed and many churches are attempting to change to respond to the new challenges. Children are growing up in a very different world from the one we experienced as children. We are inundated by information, often research based, which tells us what is best for children: how to be successful, what to eat, how to discipline – to name just a few topics. But what is *right* for them?

What *do* we want for children's groups?

What do *they* want?

Reflection

- What is my church's view of children?
  - *Is it fair?*
  - *Does it view the child from a child's or an adult's perspective?*
  - *Is this what God wants?*

CHAPTER 5

Changing Times

Strategies for teams

Carrie

Paul describes the church as a body made up of many parts,[1] a dynamic organism that lives in relationship with God. So it is clear that we live in constantly changing times, as nothing about church or people can remain static for long. Change may sometimes feel unsettling; therefore it can be helpful to employ strategies that provide a way forward and identify solutions and next steps. Strategies can help us embrace the reality that change is here to stay!

Strategies for setting up

In Acts 6:1–6 Luke recalls an incident when the needs of a vulnerable group, in this case some widows who were short of food, were becoming pronounced. The apostles demonstrated a really good strategy for dealing with this. They called all the disciples together and asked them to choose seven people who were "full of the Spirit and wisdom", and led by Stephen – and this was only to wait on tables!

We believe that children are another minority group in church whose voices are rarely heard, but the same attitude of people being set aside to work with them should be adopted. These special people need to be filled with the Holy Spirit and wisdom; they need to be chosen by the church and commissioned in prayer for a task of the utmost responsibility – working with children.

They are to be entrusted with young lives that are precious to God. They will be working with young people who may become tomorrow's leaders.

However, too often those that end up working in the children's groups are there because they were left standing when everybody else took two swift steps backwards!

Overwhelmingly, these people tend to be women.

Often children's workers are so few that they rarely get to be part of the main congregation, and end up working with children all the time. So where do they get fellowship, and a chance to worship and be fed from the word of God?

One church[2] saw this and chose to run a midweek service especially for those working with the children, which worked very well.

In churches with lots of families, another solution is to create teams for different age groups made up of four "Teachers" who take responsibility for planning and running the sessions, and so work for one month in four. (It can be organised so that each leader works once every month, but this is far less consistent from the children's perspective and in practice it means that more errors are made in remembering who is doing which slot.) These Teachers are specially commissioned by the church.

The children's work will also need two Helpers per week, who turn up early to help prepare, focus on the children during the session, and help clear up afterwards. They might need to be reminded by the Teachers the week before.

The Helpers are people in the church who want to work with children occasionally and also *all* the parents – including all fathers present. I ran this as a non-negotiable expectation for many years and found it to be successful.

The reason I insisted on this was that we needed at least three adults per session to be safe (one adult to escort children to the washroom, and two adults with the group at any one time). I also wanted the parents to take responsibility for their own children and their spiritual input in some way. I felt that they needed to experience the children's church themselves at least once or twice a term, so that they could make connections with their children's experiences. I felt it was important for all children to experience father figures as a natural part of church. I often had to battle for this, sometimes with mothers saying they would take their husbands' turns for them. It was especially important for those reluctant dads to tune into their child in the church context. I helped them by giving them a clear role to play in the session, so they knew what to do and used their interests where possible, but I remained resolute!

In retrospect I found that some reluctant fathers, who were roped in as helpers, turned out to be the greatest assets to the teaching team later on! And others demonstrated their new learning by voluntarily coming to help clear up and do some of the heavier jobs at the end of a session, as their eyes had been opened as to the physical nature of the task.

Having a large number of Teachers and Helpers means that their turn is regular but infrequent, and so they can still remain part of the main church fellowship. This works well in a church with large numbers of families.

However, in churches with a smaller numbers of families, the aim would be to select a team that could both be committed to the group and also be on a rota so that they can be "fed and watered" and pastored in the church. So the principle remains the same: someone with overall responsibility to give continuity for the children, plus parents on a rota. If all church members are of equal importance, then employing a children's worker is also an option.

Generally the children's church team should follow the school calendar, so when the holidays come the team has a complete break. The church then needs to think of new, creative ways of providing quality input for the children as well as the adults. When the team starts back up again they will be enormously appreciated!

And now, a word about men. In our society there are many fragmented families and numerous children under the age of seven rarely encounter men as positive role models in the normal course of their lives. During these early years, sexual development in children undergoes important changes and both genders need to interact with men as well as women in order to understand who they are.

This can influence their later relationships with and attitudes to men.

When I was teaching a Reception and Year 1 class, I was concerned for the large number of children who seemed not to have many positive male role models. The school already had a grandfather figure who came and read stories to whole classes throughout the school. However, along with the head teacher, I addressed this issue further in two ways. Firstly, I was lucky enough to have a father of a child in my class, who was the main care-giver for his children, and he came in weekly for a morning to help me by running small groups in the classroom such as sewing, woodwork, cooking and reading with children. And secondly, I asked my husband, a chartered accountant working locally, to bring his guitar in for a weekly singing session. He came in his business suit! What I can vividly remember was the group of children, mostly made up of those with absent dads, sitting as close to Neil as possible, right up to his knees, with focused attention and appreciating any encouragement that came their way. They seemed hungry for affirmation.

Children need to experience both male and female role models in church, in order to give them a complete picture (in other care settings the workers will be predominantly female). This also reflects God in his fullness:[3]

> *So God created humankind*
> *in his image,*
> *in the image of God*
> *he created them;*
> *male and female*
> *he created them.*

Please do make sure that all adults who will be working with children and parents are "police checked" for child protection reasons. In the UK this is a legal obligation. Legal requirements vary from country to country, so please make sure you know what is legally expected of you.

Strategies for gathering a team

The greatest children's resources that any church has are the adults that are part of it. Any practical resources come a very poor second; the adults are vital.

It is important for the whole team to meet together at the beginning of the year, in order to recognize that each member of the team is of equal value and should feel that they belong. Each person who is involved with the children at church is very important because they will be touching children's lives. Children are also very sensitive to our attitudes to individual adults and so all need to be fully acknowledged. Some people shy away from involvement as they are "just a helper", but with children nobody is "just" anything, they are all significant. It could be they are actually worried about getting more drawn in, in which case reassure them that there is no ulterior motive of more responsibility coming their way, but everybody's input is of value and the team need to grow together.

Starting with our strengths

If feasible, arrange a time for the team to meet in a comfortable setting and with food, in whatever way is culturally relevant. Ask each to contribute ideas of something they enjoy doing with children, and accept anything!

Write it down.

I have found such rich talents to draw on over the years: singing, storytelling, playing instruments, providing creative resources, cooking/making food, acting out stories, sharing pets, dancing, circle games, talking and listening to children, reading stories one to one, joining in sand/water play, science experiments!

Communicate clearly with each individual to emphasize how valuable their contribution is, and encourage them by ensuring that when you are planning their session with children, you draw on these strengths and weave in their interest, whatever is written on the programme. This is a good principle because there is nothing as infectious as somebody sharing their passion.

A Bible story can use many vehicles for expression. Share what you enjoy. I have had team members get "making food such as sandwiches or biscuits" into almost any story in the Bible!

Does that matter? Well, what did the children get out of it? That needs to be our guiding light. In our group the children loved the sessions with this leader, she was relaxed and happy, and they were highly motivated by the food. (On the other hand, if I had had to "do" food with the children, the atmosphere would have been much more fraught!)

Communicate clearly with each person that you appreciate their individual contribution and all the hard work, time and energy they put into the children's work, whatever their age. Let them know that they can call on you for help with ideas. At the end of a term say "thank you" for specific things they contributed. A small written card of appreciation can help them feel valued.

I remember an occasion when I overheard somebody say to their leader, "When you criticize me you are specific, but when you praise me you generalize."

That is a good point; we need to be specific in our praise so that it is genuine.

Aims and values

It is vital at some point for the team to state what their vision is for this age group of children at church, at this time. The questions that need to be answered are:

- What do we want for our children?
- What are our values?
- What are our aims?

What do we *really* want for our children in this church, and what does it look like for this age group?

The diversity of opinions apparent even in a small team can be surprising and can explain why it sometimes feels like we have been pulling in different directions.

Ask others in the group if there are any questions that they would like addressed. If they come under a different heading such as resources, use of the room or communication between the team members etc., then keep a note to address these later on or in another team session. Already there will be food for thought.

Having had the discussion about your values and aims, try to craft them into some pithy bullet points and keep checking back with the team to achieve a consensus.

The next step is to meet with the church leadership and share this vision, which might need further discussion before being agreed by all.

Lastly, your vision can be displayed for the church to see and could go in the "Welcome" letter to new families of children entering children's church.[4] Naturally, the vision should be referred to during subsequent team meetings and should inform future developments. In due course it might need revising.

Strategies for leading a team

When teams are formed, there are typical dynamics that occur. It is helpful to know what these are in advance because then it does not come as such a surprise when a stormy time happens, for example. Here are the stages of team development, as outlined by Jillian Rodd:[5]

Stage 1: Connecting – getting together as a team

This is where a group of people become aware that they will be working together or a new member joins. Group morale can be difficult to manage, as there will be concerns about:

- Do I belong?
- Am I being included?

Team members in this phase will tend to be unwilling to disclose weaknesses. They will keep feelings hidden, will have little concern for others and are unlikely to listen effectively, as their own needs will be dominating their attention.

The leader needs to look at the task and relationships in order to enable people to feel comfortable and effective, and to provide clear direction and guidelines related to the vision and values. There will tend to be a high level of conformity in this period with few challenges! The leader can help them get to know each other through social activities, sharing food and being personally available to them.

Tasks need to be structured activities such as information sharing, organizing roles and responsibilities, and setting goals – which are important because they alleviate apprehension about change and anxiety about their competence to do the job.

Later, when the group feels moderately comfortable with each other, a degree of risk-taking occurs, such as challenging aspects of the task or the expertise of others. This heralds the transition to the next phase, when the honeymoon is over!

Stage 2: Confronting conflict in the team

The next step which occurs is inevitable, normal and healthy: it is conflict. Conflict in the team can clear the way for more productive and cooperative ways of working and can stimulate new ideas, growth and change.

Ignoring or avoiding conflict will hinder the team's progress and can even lead to the team getting stuck in a cycle of conflict which is not only distinctly unpleasant to be a part of but also reduces the team's effectiveness.

Given that conflict is a normal part of the work experience, how are we going to handle it? It is the way it is approached and managed that matters. The leader needs to use active listening skills and follow issues through to resolution.

In teams where conflict and confrontation are not resolved, decision-making and problem-solving is poor and most of the energy goes into rounds of conflict rather than being channelled into the job. Also the commitment becomes low and members can't enjoy being part of the group. As members experience raised levels of stress, some will later choose to leave, and so the team returns to the "connecting" stage again.

We also need to consider the children within all of this.

Very young children are well able to pick up on atmospheres. They would not be able to verbalize this, but they certainly respond.

Stage 3: Cooperating as a team

Here the group is cooperating and working together and some important issues will have been worked through. Team members are willing to take risks and experiment with new practices. There is good information sharing and there are win–win attitudes to problem solving, and task-related activities are anchored in a new level of trust. The team members trust themselves in the job and each other. Change has begun.

There is a good team spirit; people are more open minded, more willing to listen to and support each other. The focus is on the needs of the group rather than their own needs.

Often there is light-hearted humour. There are fewer conflicts, and when they do occur, they are less threatening and handled differently.

The leader needs to use skill in decision-making and problem-solving, using a democratic style of leadership and delegation so that responsibility is shared. Leaders should promote consensus and cooperation, and a willingness to identify and address potential problems is essential. There needs to be open communication, constructive feedback and an acknowledgment of contributions to the team. The team now takes pride in its achievements.

Stage 4: Collaborating as an effective team

The leader needs to guide the team through to this phase, where it is now functioning effectively and the leadership style is decided according to the situation. All the team members make a unique but equal contribution to the task and share responsibility with the leader. Regular review and evaluation occur so that there can be a constant cycle of improving on previous best practice. The whole team becomes solutions focused. Change is anticipated and planned for. There is an increased sense of pride in the team's achievements. The relationships are good, as there is mutual respect and support, warmth, friendliness and concern for each other. The team recognizes interdependence as well as independence. People can agree to disagree. The team is working efficiently and its members are enjoying their work. The energies of the team can spread further afield and it becomes outward looking.

> I have been part of this process in successfully designing, planning and hosting several large conferences for Bristol with a diverse and sizeable team, and also writing this book with one other person. At times like these, working is an absolute joy!

The leader can relax and leads the team in regular cycles of self-evaluation, asking:

- How are we doing?
- Where do we want to go next?
- What are our needs now?

Stage 5: Closure

This occurs when a team finishes or when a team member leaves, and it is a stage too often ignored. Actually, the members need to celebrate or mourn the ending of a team, in order to give some form of closure. It involves disengaging from the task and separating from working relationships.

- "Remember when Kate was here? She would have known what to do."
- "Didn't we work well together before all the changes?"

Comments like those above can be little indications that closure or coming to terms with changes have not been complete.

If the team has had a good history, there need to be celebrations of individual performance, task performance and relationships.

The wide range of emotional responses needs to be acknowledged. People may be angry about the team breaking up, or happy with its achievements.

If the team hasn't achieved well or has had difficult relationships, there is even more reason for good closure through evaluation by looking at each team member's contribution and what the problems were in the team. This can therefore lead to a basis for planning the next team.

Inevitably, during this period there will be a lower quality of performance. The leader needs to focus on the team's social and emotional needs in order to prepare for the establishment of the new team.

It is interesting to note some of the same team dynamics amongst the disciples that Jesus had to deal with. In Stage 2, mentioned above, there is often conflict and jostling for position. We see this in the Gospel incident where the disciples were arguing amongst themselves as to who was the greatest.[6] Jesus gave them a brilliant visual aid: he called to a child and had him (or her) stand amongst them. I can just visualize them looking down on the child and being amazed and dumbfounded as they somehow tried to understand how they were meant to humble themselves like a little child.

Another time, when Jesus sent the disciples out[7] to preach and heal the sick, they were obviously at Stage 4 when they were collaborating well.

And another time, in the wider team, two followers were on the road to Emmaus,[8] talking with deep disappointment: "… but we had hoped that he was the one who was going to redeem Israel."

Obviously they were mourning the loss of a leader in whom they had invested such hope. They had no closure (Stage 5) – just grief.

Strategies for reflecting as a team

How do you eat an elephant? In bite-sized pieces!

At certain times, maybe once or twice a year, it is important to be able to reflect as a team in order to improve the quality of all that is offered to children. Providing quality is not static but a dynamic process, involving a journey of *continually improving on your previous best* provision for children.[9] We can never say that we have arrived and there is nothing left to improve upon, or that our practice is perfect.

This is an exciting challenge, a dialogue that never grows stale.

Children are individuals and so our responsiveness to their individual needs and the challenges that come our way should provoke us to reflective action.

Reflection as a team ought to involve as many of the people who are with the children as possible – everybody is important enough to come, as each person's perceptions are valuable and unique.

An ideal way to begin is to provide comfortable surroundings and food to share, or whatever is appreciated and helps people to feel at ease.

I have used self-evaluation methods many times with schools and nurseries, as well as at children's church, and found them to be an excellent tool for improving the quality for children, provided it keeps children at the heart of all discussions and decisions and also gives a voice to everybody involved.

Circles of reflection: Reflection leading to action

Centre

Go to the middle of the diagram.

The heart throughout this process is the child. Imagine the children in your group and keep them central to your thinking.

Inner circle: What has gone well?

Start at the top of the inner circle.

Thinking of the children in your group, what has gone well? Or what aspects of the session are going well? (E.g. the children seem to enjoy coming to children's church.)

Inner circle: How do we know?

Move round the inner circle to the bottom.

What evidence do we have for our evaluation, based on the "children's many languages"? (E.g. at the allotted time, some of the children run out of the main meeting to get to their room. Others arrive and separate happily from their parent/carer. During the session they are largely engaged in what is provided for them. At the end of a session they are reluctant to leave, as they are engrossed in their self-chosen activity.)

Keep going round this circle and enable discussion.

Use a large flip chart sheet to record all contributions.

Make sure that you are careful to write down every suggestion that is offered, even if you don't agree with it.

The hidden message here is that everyone's opinion is equally valued.

Encourage discussion and comment.

The value of this discussion is dependent on its depth and content and on contributions from every member of the team, so do not rush this stage.

If quieter people need drawing out, sensitively direct a question to them or ask them to reflect on what has gone on before. It is very important that every

CIRCLES OF REFLECTION

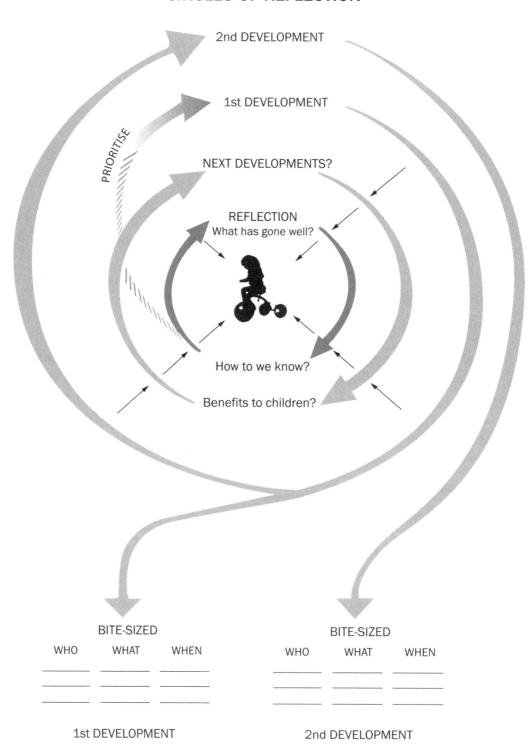

adult contributes, as each person is hugely important to the children and *does* influence them.

Everybody matters because each person interacts with the children.

Each individual will have different perceptions and interests and so their contribution is a vital part of the whole. If there is one experienced leader, it is also important that they hold back and let others speak, as this is not a one-woman/man band. This is part of the process where the team begins to develop a shared language and vision, and if it is just one person's voice, then it is not really a team.

Middle circle: What shall we develop next?

At the appropriate time, move along the dotted line to the top of the next circle layer and ask the question above.

This can be anything to develop or improve upon that will benefit the children directly, in your group. Encourage contributions and listen closely for perceptive insights. List them as bullet points.

Then prioritize the bullet points, setting out the developments by agreement. (E.g. the story part of the session has a mixed response from the children, with fidgeting and comments such as "Can we go now?" Therefore we want to develop a resource that can enhance story participation with the children. We shall get a builder's tray, sand, rocks, and some small-world people. [See the "Builder's tray" grid below.])

Middle circle: If we carry out this development, how will the children benefit?

Move round the middle circle to the bottom.

How the children will benefit is something that is harder to articulate clearly, but vital. Therefore, stay with this, listen closely for perceptive insights. The reasoning here of how the children will benefit, changes the possible development from a bright idea to one that has depth of purpose to positively impact children. It gives me the fire in my belly to follow it through, because I am fighting for quality for the children.

If there is no clear benefit for the children, and it's just a good idea, then it does not belong here. The focus needs to begin and end with the children.

Start with: "The children will benefit by…" (E.g. the children will benefit by being able to join in with the story in a physical and interactive way, using more of their senses. They will also be able to access the tray throughout the session to rehearse the story, and explore their feelings along with other children.)

Keep going round this circle and enable discussion.

Outer circle: Who will do what, by when?

At the appropriate time, move along the dotted line to the top of the next outer circle layer and ask the above question.

Break the development that has been agreed on into bite-sized pieces. There can be many tasks to one development. Ask everybody to get their diary out. Acknowledge that you all have exciting and full lives outside of this group. Allow each member to volunteer, but generally no more than once. Ask them to be realistic rather than ambitious as to what they will do by when. Expect everybody to contribute something, and they will generally choose something they enjoy or find easy. Do not allow one person to take on many actions – you want to build a team by sharing the responsibility out.

A builder's tray – an example of a group development

WHO	WILL DO WHAT	BY WHEN
Fiona	Will find a builder's tray left after building works at home.	14 Oct
Greg	Will bring silver sand from excess at home.	14 Oct
Sam	Will research catalogues for small-world people (different diversity/age) and will tell Maya.	1 Oct
Maya	Will buy small-world people in her next order.	7 Oct
Jiwan	Will bring rocks, peat, evergreen branches from garden.	14 Oct
Kairen	Will ask friends for small-world animals.	10 Oct
Carrie	Will check on all the above and will email team progress and the start date of the builder's tray going live!	14 Oct

One person then needs to take responsibility to check with each person that the small task has been achieved, and if not, to offer help.

Continue with other developments, but aim realistically rather than taking on too much at one time.

The cycle is now complete.

When the development has been carried out, there is such satisfaction on having made a contribution so that everybody involved feels a sense of ownership. You can see the work of your hands, the fruit of your labour, and the joy of seeing the children's experience enhanced is incredible.

After a period of time, carrying out various reflections that have led to actions with the team, you will cast your mind back to your starting point and be amazed at the enormous changes that have happened.

Budget

The following approach works well when seeking a budget or communicating with the leadership or other interested parties with whom you want to engage:

1. What do we do well?
2. How do we know?
3. What do we want to develop next?
4. If this development happens, the children benefit by…?
5. In order to achieve this (Who will do what by when?):

   we will do…

   we need you to…

Although this might sound simplistic, I have genuinely found this approach to practically work in extraordinary ways. Mountains have been moved!

Strategies for a child-centred church calendar

Children need to remain very clearly our main focus throughout any planning involving the church calendar, rather than church traditions riding roughshod over their needs.

Wherever possible, we need to try to step into the children's shoes and see their experience of church through their eyes.

Nobody can claim to see through the eyes of a child, but understanding their home context, their developmental needs and tuning in to their many languages can give us strong clues.

Church traditions can be held very dear by many of our church family, and that needs to be respected. However, we also need to be prepared to be advocates for children, speaking on their behalf where they are not able. If we are to speak for them, we also need to be creative in offering solutions to provide win–win outcomes for everybody, as far as possible.

Christmas!

This can be a wonderful time of year, with the whole church joining in and contributing to the celebrations.

Often each children's age group in church is required to perform in some way. However, this is more appropriate for older ages.

Keeping the children as our focus, we need to look at what is required for the youngest children to perform a song or part of a story.

In order for a three-year-old child to learn a song, this would have to be repeated many times over several weeks. So for something totally new, rehearsals would have to start in November. At the actual performance, when faced with an audience, three year olds tend to go silent.

In order to rehearse a play, practices would have to go on for even longer than a song, maybe starting in October. The individual child's experience of rehearsing over that period of time might be best described as boring – that is, a lot of sitting around with a couple of the children doing much more.

Listening to what young children want and who they want to be in, say, the Nativity story will elicit many Marys.

And why not?

Every child is special.

Every child wants that feeling of significance.

There may be many angels, possibly some kings and shepherds and the odd extraneous animal, even African ones. One of my group wanted to be the biscuit – the biscuit that Mary gave to the donkey, of course!

So, what is really central to Christmas?

It is about that shared Nativity story, about the amazing gift of Jesus, God's Son, coming as a baby. This is best communicated interactively at the children's level, in their small group, around December time, so that it stays fresh. At this age the best acting or retelling of a story is where every child gets to act every part that they want to, sometimes all at the same time – e.g. taking turns to ride on the back of the donkey (a willing adult); knocking on doors to be told "No room here" until the right one is opened; looking at a real baby (brought in by a parent) to show that Jesus was human but also God's Son; opening presents.

Christmas is also about taking part, so anything to share can be video-recorded and played at the packed service, such as a song, children playing with Nativity figures and discussing the story amongst themselves, or children dressing up as some characters in a previous Sunday School session (assuming the correct permissions have been given). And a new song learned can be sung together with everybody in the service.

On the actual day all children are invited to come dressed up as whoever they want to be (many Marys, maybe!) and take part in the service by sitting with their families, or in their group if they are happy to, as all the excitement can be overwhelming. There will also be extra clothes provided by the children's church for those who have forgotten, so that none is left out.

If there are a couple of children who would love a more formal role of reading something out or acting, then an adult can support them in this and practise outside of church time, so the rest of the group is not expected to sit silently and watch any rehearsals. In this way, no child is set up to fail or to sit still for weeks on end. Instead, the awe and wonder of the birth of Jesus can continue to give that frisson of excitement through our shared experience and in a way that is appropriate to all.

These principles can be applied to any of the church festivals:

- What does the celebration involve?
- What is the quintessence of the Bible truth?
- What can the children join in with that is developmentally appropriate?
- What alternative ways are there for children to contribute to or benefit from this festival?

- What will be the main messages that the children take away with them?
- Is what is planned inclusive for all?

Mother's Day and Father's Day

In this generation we are more aware of the variance in family structures, and many children in our churches grow up in different family configurations. These could be: single parents; same-sex parents; reconstituted families with many step-siblings; grandparents or nannies as the main caregivers; adopted children; as well as the traditional mother and father and 2.4 children.

Any celebrations we hold should be completely inclusive and hold a mirror up to each type of family so that they can recognize themselves and see that they belong here. This is another example of the power of hidden messages.

We also need to be respectful of our multicultural society, with different traditions which we need to be sensitive to and incorporate where possible.

As described in Chapter 6, I have celebrated Mother's Day with my group of children in a meaningful and relevant way. This was inclusive to all those present and there was no expectation for the children to make something that was my idea. However, if a child in that group had lost a mother through death or family breakdown, then for the sake of that child I would avoid that subject with the group.

Reflecting together in teams can bring clarity of purpose and a strengthening of skills. Working in teams will always include coping with change. Changing times can appear superficially to be unsettling, but they can also be exciting, ripe with potential and dynamic opportunities for new ideas, and beneficial to all.

As James Baldwin, the Civil Rights activist, said: "Not everything that is faced can be changed. But nothing can be changed until it is faced."[10]

May we have the courage, for the sake of our children, to meet this challenge.

Reflection

- What are the benefits of having men involved in the work with very young children?

  - *What are some of the prejudices they might face from our church members?*

- How are children's workers recruited in my church?

- Who pastors the children's workers?

- If I could pick my dream team in church, who would it involve?

  - *Is there any way of getting them involved even for a short time, e.g. playing the guitar for ten minutes?*

- Reflect on a time when there was conflict at home or in another situation where there were children who picked up on the atmosphere.

  - *How did you know they had picked up on the bad atmosphere?*

  - *What did they do?*

  - *How did they alter?*

- Consider the team you are currently part of and try to decide whereabouts in the process of team development you are.

  - *What evidence have you got for this?*

  - *What are some of the characteristics?*

CHAPTER 6

Time Out!

Are there ever any "nevers"?

Carrie

Well, there might be! However, for every "never" there are creative solutions with the children's best interests at heart.

It is often said that if people use the words "never" and "always" in terms of relationships, then it shuts down the possibility of positive communication. This is because it fastens behaviours and past events to the person rather than letting them move on. It is also extreme language and is generally not describing the whole picture accurately. This guidance may well be true in terms of relational dialogue. However, in this context, the "nevers" refer to practices that we choose to use with children and the boundaries we set ourselves.

When considering the wide range of activities we can choose from to present to children, then there are certainly activities that are unhelpful and would best be avoided.

There are boundaries that we stick to in all our involvement with children that have come out of years of working with them, listening closely to them and reflecting on any possible hidden messages. This has been part of our ongoing dialogue with colleagues, accompanied by reading current theories and research, as we try to give young children the very best quality provision. This reflective thinking is something that needs to continue throughout our involvement with children.

In church provision for children, we are long overdue in calling "Time out!" on antiquated practices that need to be relegated to the bench permanently.

"It never did me any harm" is a common response, when change is suggested.

If I hadn't revisited the health advice that had been around when I was little, my daughter would probably be heavily scarred today. As a six month old,

Rebecca was being held on a friend's lap and grabbed a freshly poured cup of black coffee, which spilled all over her body. Using the current/updated advice at the time, I quickly plunged her into a sink full of cold running water for fifteen minutes (the advice is now twenty minutes). Thankfully, she emerged completely unscarred, and recovered from the shock and pain in due course. Had I followed the advice around when I was a child, which was to rub butter into the burn, then the outcome would have been very different. Although health advice and educational advice have different expressions, they are both still important, and both impact lives, some more visibly than others.

Never give children adult-drawn outlines/worksheets to colour in

A printed or adult-drawn outline communicates strongly to children that this is *exactly* how you draw, for example, a flower and shuts down their creativity and eats away at their self-confidence. We covered this with the "lamb" example earlier in Chapter 2.

I believe adult-drawn outlines can seriously damage children's creative health. How is this conclusion drawn?

By watching children closely and "listening" to their language and behaviour over a period of time. Giving children worksheets or templates to draw round often causes responses such as: "I don't know how to draw… Can you draw it for me?… I can't do it…"

Continuing observation of children shows a gradual reduction in self-initiated drawing.

Teachers and researchers are agreed on this issue and have been for some time.

Worksheets have not been used in good current practice for many years and certainly not with children aged seven and under.

Why have worksheets been given in the first place?

- Is it to give the children something to do at a point in the session?

Solution! Give the children a selection of blank sheets of paper and pencils etc. to choose from, that actually work and are satisfying to use. This means that children can grow in confidence, developing their own creative expressions. Also, in my experience, when I have compared my artistic attempts to those of most three to seven year olds, I genuinely think theirs are superior (as in the case of the lamb).

- Is it to communicate to parents the theme of the session?

Solution! Write a note on the door for parents to read as they collect their children or send a note home with each child.

- Is it to underline the theme of the session?

Solution! Find something that the children can take part in that is more meaningful and interactive for them. This could be involving children in making and eating sandwiches after the story of Jesus feeding the 5,000, or playing with water and sand after hearing about the foolish man building his house on the sand.

The real reason for the use of worksheets is that adults find it hard to let go of them. Like cigarette smoking, worksheets can be seen as an unhealthy addiction which is painful to give up in the short term, as they are a habit and a prop. There is an uncomfortable withdrawal phase which, if navigated successfully, can result in fresh breaths of freedom and a wide-open vista of creative possibilities.

Never make children work on a production line

Such as identical "daffodils" made out of egg-boxes, that the adult has designed beforehand, to be created by the end of the session.

This sort of activity would be appropriate if we wanted to prepare children for adulthood on a factory line. Or we wanted to stamp out individual expression and creativity. There is little joy in receiving these as a parent. It can train the children to follow instructions without thinking and is actually a fairly meaningless task. So it is hard to find the benefit for the children.

Observing children as they follow a list of instructions has shown that their language shuts down and their anxiety levels rise. At this stage of child development we should be encouraging their thinking skills. As they are involved in creating, say, their own junk model, they will be using their senses of touch, sight and smell. They will also be drawing on memories from past experiences, making decisions, exploring texture and goodness of fit, and reflecting on and revising plans. Often children show high levels of involvement and absorption in this type of self-directed activity and can concentrate for prolonged periods of time.

This is why the *process* is much more important than the product.

So, let's look at why the "production line" situation might arise.

- It's Mother's Day (and all the children present have a mother) and the mothers will expect something from the session.

Solution! Have a discussion with the group about things they like doing with their mum and have a helper write down (quickly) what any child volunteers. Then provide free choice of activities. Any child that has not contributed in a group can be chatted to, one to one, whilst playing in the rest of the session, and any comments should be written down. The adult with the neatest writing, using sticky labels, writes what has been said by each child and sticks the label onto any created piece or on a piece of card. The child can then present to their mother something that is meaningful and relevant. In my experience this has been received with expressions of delight and sometimes tears of emotion.

- Adults expect a product as a sign that their child has learned something in the session.

Solution! This assumption needs to be challenged at some point by clear communication to parents and leaders and may be part of the welcome letter (see Chapter 10). Do the adults come out of church having made a thumb pot?!

In the meantime, if parents ask, "What have they made today?" you can respond, "Today it is in their heads, not their hands!"

Never "label" children

Both negative and positive "labels" can become self-fulfilling prophecies or straitjackets – for example: Andrew is always clumsy, Amie is the naughty one, Jennifer is the good one, Nasim is the sporty one (read Jennifer Rees Larcombe about the negative power of being labelled "good").[1]

We believe as Christians that words are powerful and effective. "God said, 'Let there be light,' and there was light."[2] We too can have a powerful effect by speaking authoritatively over children.

It is common to hear children in church being described as "naughty" or "challenging", as a way of communicating amongst adults. This is such a disservice to children and their families.

> I have had parents in a state of high anxiety, nearly in tears themselves, rush up to me at the end of a session asking, "Did he behave himself this time?" In that particular instance, of course, he was happy because he had been given appropriate and interesting opportunities.

There can be behaviour issues which need to be addressed, and this is covered in Chapter 10. However, these are young children and need to be given a fresh start every day, just like we hope for from our heavenly Father.

A very real risk in using these labels is that our expectations of a child heavily influence their behaviour and competency, rather than the other way round.

> This is supported by some interesting research of secondary school children. A group of black children were taken as a sample, and were performing well below average. They were monitored and their teachers were given instructions by the research team. Various teachers were told that the child in their class from the sample group was performing poorly in their class but performing very well in several other classes (this was untrue). The result was that the teacher's expectation of the child's ability rose, which altered the interaction between the teacher and the child, and then the child's actual performance changed dramatically for the better. The child's measured performance changed to well above average. This was repeated in a wide study sample. So the *only* thing that had changed was the teacher's expectation.

Hence the power of labels! Labels then influence expectations and the cycle is complete.

One type of label is still prevalent today, and that is gender stereotyping. In church we need to really embrace the truth that there is "neither male nor female"[3] in God's hierarchy, but we are equal in his sight. Language that attributes activity preferences to gender does our children a disservice.

> I introduced an open-plan house for "small-world play" (i.e. a "doll's house") and put carefully chosen play families in it which covered a range of ages and skin colour, along with some furniture. There were many predictions amongst

the adults that day that the girls would like it. I decided to do a simple checklist and found that it was used in *equal* measure by boys and girls throughout the session.

This small-world play is important as it gives our children a chance to imagine, replay and interact with situations and other children in a dynamic and creative way. They need to do so with freedom and confidence, uninhibited by subtle stereotypical communication that this is somehow a feminine thing to do.

It is true that boys and girls develop at different rates and that their brains also show a gender difference, but there is no need to straitjacket children into extreme roles when they have tremendous potential to develop in unique ways. The full aspects of their personality and skills need a fertile soil in which to grow with confidence, so that girls can be free to develop muscular strength and physical ability, and boys can be gentle and nurturing.

- How do I speak to a child without labelling them?

Solution! Always separate the behaviour from the child. For example: "That was a thoughtful and kind thing to do… I noticed that you really love running fast… You might find it easier to use both hands to hold the jug while you are pouring… I need to move this heavy box; who is feeling strong today?" (*Not* "Can some strong boys help me?")

- How do I say something positive to a child who habitually is disruptive?

Solution! Catch them doing something positive and affirm that, however small it is.

Never force children to do what they don't want to do

Church should be a safe place where, above all else, every person, including the little ones, is given honour and respect. Children often do not have the language skills to express why they might be feeling uncomfortable about joining in a group session, but they can often indicate their preference clearly.

Some children need to be able to be spectators for a considerable time before joining in. Others love to jump right into new experiences.

Children in the Way?

Adults are just the same!

Just as adults make choices about joining in aspects of church and often observe for a while first (many months!), so do children. When we give genuine choice, the hidden message is: "I value what you choose. I am listening to you and I respect your decision."

For example, I was running an ambitious session where the children had the opportunity to do foot painting, which obviously involved taking off their socks and shoes, stepping in paint and then walking around on large sheets of paper. Then they could sit on a chair to have their feet washed with perfumed soap, dried with fluffy towels and talcum powdered. It was a fun session and all the children were offered turns both with the painting and with the foot washing (linked to Jesus' foot washing!), as well as the usual activities. Most of the children chose to take an active part but there were some who were happier watching this unusual event, before involving themselves in something more familiar.

That's absolutely fair enough!

All the children in the session enjoyed themselves. We were careful not to over-encourage them, thus giving the hidden message that "it is better to join in", which usually serves to make children put their brakes on. Instead we gave them genuine freedom to choose. This approach led to a peaceful and absorbed session.

Let's look at this scenario:

- A child does not want to leave their parent and join in with the group.

Solution! The parent should join the group with the child for as many sessions as it takes for the child to feel confident enough to be left. The child needs to decide the timeline and have a happy experience. If both parents come to church, then the father should take his fair share of turns, as this is not just a female role. From the child's point of view, this outing to church is once a week – which is a very long period when you are, for example, three years old – and it can take a considerable time for church to feel like a familiar part of their weekly pattern.

Never get cross over mistakes or when things go wrong

Children are often very good observers and in a group there are many pairs of eyes focused on the powerful adult who is leading or helping in a session. When something goes wrong, the way we react and respond will be noticed with interest.

One of the strongest messages we give is through modelling – that is, how we behave, rather than what we tell someone to do.

- I find mistakes hard to handle. How should I approach this in the group?

Solution! See unforeseen events as opportunities for learning something else, something that wasn't planned. Put your original plan on hold and calmly narrate what has happened and ask questions as to how to find a solution. Involve the children where possible; allow them to resolve the problem with you. Then reassess whether it is still appropriate to return to your original plan. The lesson taught here can be really important: *When mistakes happen, they can be sorted out, and it's not the end of the world!*

Never set children up for failure

The feeling of failure can be all consuming for us as adults. It might be helpful to reflect on a recent situation where you failed and others witnessed it.

Stay with that feeling a while and try to step into children's shoes, in their world where they are learning a new language, how to move their bodies, how to relate to people of all ages outside of the family, where many people around them are bigger, stronger, faster, understand more and make most of the decisions.

In order to be able to grow as children they need the confidence to try new things, have new experiences and express themselves without feeling ridiculed, laughed at or told they are cute or that they have got it wrong.

- What is the best approach to avoid these pitfalls?

Solution! Have realistic, child-centred expectations. The way to understand what these might be is to observe the children and notice what interests them. Then with this as a starting point, build a session around that.

Provide materials and resources that are enticing.

Have a look at your children's church from a child's viewpoint and examine what you already provide for them. For example, would you want to sit on the cushions that they sit on? No? Well, get rid of them. Their sense of smell is keener than yours!

What about the resources that are generally available for children's mark-making? Are they accessible and do they work? It is better to have six colour pencils that work rather than a box full of odds and ends where children's efforts will be frustrated by the time they find the one pencil that is sharp enough.

- Children don't know the answers to all the questions I am going to ask, so they are bound to get some wrong. Is that OK?

Solution! Do not ask questions that have only one right answer.

Don't test them!

Instead, ask children genuine questions.

Ask questions that you don't know the answer to and be delighted and respectful with the response. For example, with the lost sheep, having explored the story together, some questions could be: "I wonder why the sheep got lost? Have you ever been lost? Have you lost a special toy? Then what happened? How do you think the shepherd felt?" In my experience with this story, if I just ask, "Have you ever been lost? What did it feel like?", I get some very animated conversations that last for a considerable time. Then the point of the story is that God finds you, just like the shepherd found his sheep.

Once again, it is the *process* that is important – in this case the thinking process – rather than being able to regurgitate something learnt by rote.

Never make empty threats or empty promises

Phrases such as: "If you don't behave, I'll take you back to your parents!… You wouldn't like your parents to know… What will everybody think of you?… It will be your turn next week" (it's easy to forget).

This is essentially a question of trust. We need to be true to our word so that children learn that when we talk about truths we mean it, and when we promise something we mean that as well. They also need to feel secure, and empty words are confusing and can make them more unsettled.

Are we attributing too much intelligence to very young children?

Our experience has taught us that children are much more finely tuned than most people give them credit for. Children might not be able to articulate what reasons they have for feeling uncomfortable with a certain adult but they are actually often extremely perceptive, sometimes more so than adults!

- If I can't use language like that, then what do I say?

Solution! This is an important issue to think through before the need arises. If new boundaries need to be set, then decide on these beforehand and calmly draw on them when appropriate. However, we should first examine our own expectations of children carefully and be willing to adapt to their needs. I believe I am there to serve and give children the very best quality that I can (rather than: they are there to fit into my plans).

Never humiliate children

It is easy to humiliate children, particularly in a church setting. This might be because there is often an interlude when the adults are talking for long periods after the formal meeting is over, and children can get rowdy. So it is all too easy to reprimand them publicly. Adults can also use the technique of humiliation as a way of controlling a group. However, it is never right to try to shame a child in this way. It can even be disguised as laughing at them, which might appear fine to the adult but the child can be mortified by it.

- My child is often deliberately naughty when I am trying to clear up after a session and they are running around with their friends. Surely I need to set proper boundaries?

Solution! When this situation occurs, quietly go over to your child, remove them gently from the group and when you are alone with them, get down on their eye level and calmly discuss the issue with them. Take time to invite them to comment, and listen closely. Be prepared to adapt your plan by taking them into account but also enable them to help you meet your requirements as well. If they are bored, then suggest ways they and their friends can help you in your task. If you give them a little bit of responsibility, they may enjoy the job and even become your co-worker. Rejoin the group, keeping their confidence as to what has taken place between you, because that is private and confidential.

As Paul says in 1 Corinthians: "Everything is permissible... but not everything is beneficial... [or]... constructive."[4]

So it is with giving ourselves guidelines.

If we base our course of action on current best practice, in accordance with professionals in the field and our ongoing dependence on God, our work with children will be enhanced. And I believe that giving the children in our care the very best quality we can and serving them to our utmost ability is actually serving God and is part of our spiritual worship.

I also think that our work with children in these early years of their lives is a time of sowing seeds, some of which bear fruit immediately, while others take years to reveal their full-grown produce.

Let's make sure the seed that we sow is good.

Reflection

- Are there any situations with children in my church which make me feel slightly uncomfortable?
  - *Why do you think this is?*
  - *What action could be taken to change this positively for the children?*
- Are there certain children that struggle with a particular aspect of a Sunday morning?
  - *Why do you think this is?*
  - *Working from the child's point of view, what simple changes could be made to enable those children to have a better experience?*
- Can you remember when you last made a mistake or did something wrong that others noticed?
  - *What led to this incident?*
  - *How did others respond?*
  - *How did you respond?*
  - *What would have helped to redeem the situation?*
  - *How could you use this experience in a relevant way for children?*
- Can you remember a time when you were humiliated in front of others?
  - *Where were you?*
  - *What happened?*
  - *How did you feel?*
  - *How can you use that negative experience and make it positive by deciding what you would do when relating to a child in a similar situation?*

No Way. The Hundred Is There.
(The Hundred Languages of Children)

This poem by Loris Malaguzzi beautifully conveys the important roles that imagination and discovery play in early childhood learning. Much of Reggio Emilia philosophy is based on protecting children from becoming subjected too early to institutionalized doctrines which often make learning a chore rather than an extension of natural curiosity.

The child is made of one hundred.
The child has
a hundred languages
a hundred hands
a hundred thoughts
a hundred ways of thinking
of playing, of speaking.
A hundred.
Always a hundred
ways of listening
of marvelling, of loving
a hundred joys
for singing and understanding
a hundred worlds
to discover
a hundred worlds
to invent
a hundred worlds
to dream.
The child has
a hundred languages
(and a hundred hundred hundred more)
but they steal ninety-nine.
The school and the culture
separate the head from the body.
They tell the child:
to think without hands
to do without head
to listen and not to speak
to understand without joy
to love and to marvel

only at Easter and at Christmas.
They tell the child:
to discover the world already there
and of the hundred
they steal ninety-nine.
They tell the child:
that work and play
reality and fantasy
science and imagination
sky and earth
reason and dream
are things
that do not belong together.
And thus they tell the child
that the hundred is not there.
The child says:
No way. The hundred is there.

Loris Malaguzzi,
Founder of the Reggio Emilia Approach
(translated by Lella Gandini)[1]

Section 3

Small but Essential for Growth

We have discussed the importance of knowing about the needs of the developing brain, the consistency of care for our youngest children and their drive to form relationships. So what does working with them *look* like?

This section looks at issues of development and good practice with children from newborn to three years old.

CHAPTER 7

Taking Time

Do you know who I am?

Isobel

> At 6.35 p.m. on Friday, 6 June 2008 I was gazing into the eyes of my first grandchild. She was minutes old and I had just watched her being born. Yes, I was overwhelmed by the miracle of this tiny new life, but most of all I wanted to get to know her.

Like most babies, she looked at my face as she tried to adjust to this big new world. The familiar voices of mum and dad must have been a comfort to her as she began her quest to find out who she is and who she is relating to. Studies have shown that babies prefer patterns that are like faces. They particularly look into the eyes of the person they are with. It is suggested that they look into eyes to see if they are OK, and if all is well and the carer is content, peaceful and happy, then they feel OK. If the carer is anxious or unhappy, then the baby does not feel that they are OK.

Is it just coincidence that the focal length of a baby is about twenty-two centimetres, the length from the crook of an arm when holding a baby to the adult's face? Or is this part of the design of a great Creator to make sure that as relational beings we are born equipped to start relationships with nurturing carers?

What does this mean for those adults who are charged with the care of infants in the crèche?

What is it that we want for these children? What are our shared beliefs, values and aims for this group? David writes in Psalm 34:11–13:

> *Come, my children, listen to me; I will teach you the fear of the Lord. Whoever of you loves life and desires to see many good days, keep your tongue from evil and your lips from speaking lies. Turn from evil and do good; seek peace and pursue it.*

Children in the Way?

The way that adults in crèche talk together about families, about other church members, about the children, will all be assimilated by the child and they will pick up the attitudes and values of those who are caring for them. These are not necessarily the agreed values of the church but the "hidden" values. Young children are not usually deaf and they are all tuned in. I often think that babies are like Sky TV satellite dishes. They pick up the airwaves that are being transmitted, but their receptors are not yet complete so their interpretation of the transmission may be inaccurate.

But they get the underlying message!

Babies very sensitively tune into the relationships and the atmospheres around them.

During the first few years of life the infant begins to discover some answers to the questions "Who am I?" and "Who are you?" They establish their various identities within different contexts and with different people. I guess we all recognize the chameleon-like way that we adapt our behaviour in different situations. Children learn about their home culture, the values and beliefs of their families and the traditions within which they are growing up. Many very young children make the transition to nursery or the childminder and start to negotiate another set of cultural expectations and beliefs – some make several different transitions.

Think how many groups, carers and different environments that a child joins within their first three years of life.

Research shows that if they are supported by consistent key people, these transitions will be less stressful; but the child is facing change.

Working with a very young child recently, who was new to nursery but already a skilful communicator in her home language, other staff were surprised that she was non-communicative verbally within the nursery and made no effort to socialize with other children. As a two year old, she watched everyone and everything closely. I don't think that she missed anything. I wonder if she was trying to piece together this jigsaw of the nursery day – the routine, the behaviour, the language, the expectations, in fact the culture of this new place. Being bilingual often includes a silent phase. This is normal.

Many very young children, when faced with a new situation, just watch, listen and wait. This is quite safe when mum or dad or the familiar person is around, but when faced with relative strangers in a busy environment, it can be scary and anyway, "Who knows me?"

There can be a real comfort in knowing that someone knows you and understands how you tick.

> I remember, as a young teenager, when I was a member of a rather staid youth group, one of the helpers said, "Izzie, I feel I understand most people but I really don't understand how you tick!" As a rebel, part of me was really pleased that she couldn't suss me out. I rather liked the idea of being a bit of an enigma, particularly to a Christian leader.
>
> But part of me felt alone. *Did* anyone understand me? I didn't understand myself. I was constantly asking myself, "Who am I?" and "What is life all about?"

I could articulate these thoughts, but what about a baby? How do they deal with uncertain adults?

Young babies need to feel that they belong and that they are known. We have already considered the findings of ongoing brain studies, but basic knowledge about the developing needs of young children, as well as knowing important information about them from their parents, is crucial for all those who care for children. It is interesting to reflect on the reassurance that the psalmist, David, gained from his belief that God knew him.

Caring for the very youngest children requires a sensitive and skilful approach. We cannot hope to replicate home-from-home, nor should we. The crèche or the nursery group in church will never be home. However, we do need to provide an appropriate social and emotional environment. Theories around attachment have been debated for many years, since John Bowlby[1] suggested that infants who do not form strong attachments with their mothers will be unable to make good relationships later in life. He was studying children and presenting his findings as the Second World War was ending. Male soldiers were returning from the front and wanting their jobs back from the women who had filled their posts through the war years. Research suggesting that women, especially mothers, should be at home was politically useful, and facilitated the swift return of mothers to their home and children, and men back into work. Bowlby's research has been challenged over the years, partly due to his insistence on the critical role of the mother. Other researchers have suggested that the baby can become attached to more than one primary carer, including siblings.

No researchers challenge the importance of attachment for the young child.

So how do we respond to this fact within church? How can we ensure that babies feel safe and can become attached to primary carers?

I think that it is important for us to remember that sixty to ninety minutes a week is a very short time in relation to the whole week, but a long time for an infant to feel insecure. Each week is like a fresh transition to an unfamiliar place unless we really think hard about how to make our crèche environments safe places.

Babies use their senses to find out about the world and make connections between the familiar and unfamiliar. Ensuring that they have their own special toy or "cuddly", using their own cups or bottles, knowing their sleep routines, their special people and phrases, their favourite rhymes and books will all help the baby to feel more secure. Above all, gentle, positive touch and handling will help to comfort a child.

It is such a shame that we have become so fearful of using touch with young children. Yes, we need to safeguard children and make all the necessary checks and take precautions to know who is with the children, but touch is essential. The right touch relays the message that "I am loved and cared for." It was reputedly Princess Diana who said that we need four hugs a day just for maintenance – the rest is a bonus!

So touch, taste and smell are all important factors in providing babies with safe and caring environments. Listening and responding are equally important. It is interesting to me that when we talk with a baby, we instinctively raise our voices and talk in what is known as "motherese", or more correctly, infant-directed speech. This pitch and tone is easier for a baby to tune in to. Again, how amazing that talking to babies this way is innate – showing that we are created to relate. It is a natural longing.

So, adults can offer a model of how to develop a relationship. Or can they? I think that developing relationships is a mutual activity and we develop a "dance" in our interactions with each other.

So we also need to "tune in" to the baby, watching their body language, the focus of their attention, when they look away, the sounds they make and their sense of ease with whatever is happening.

I was playing with a baby recently, and he was laughing and chuckling as we played "round and round the garden". Then he looked away and made it clear to me that he was no longer interested. On another occasion, a young child, only about eleven months old, remembered that we had played a chasing game the last time we had met. She signalled that she wanted to play this again by looking hard at me and then crawling away. She then stopped and waited until I got onto the floor and crawled slowly towards her saying, "I'm coming to get you!" With that she turned and crawled away at speed, relishing the moment when I would "catch her and eat her all up"!

Regular carers will get to know each baby and will be able to listen to them more effectively and know how to respond to them.

I am privileged to look after Niall (eleven months) on Mondays for the next few months as his mum returns to work. We go to Sing and Sign together after dropping his sister off at nursery. I sit with the other mothers and their babies as we go through a repertoire of songs and signs for an hour each week. Niall has definite favourites and is always excited when Jess the cat appears from the box and comes out to greet the children individually. Each child has a turn. Does Niall sit eagerly to wait his turn? No. He crawls over to other babies who have an interesting snack, a fascinating toy or a smiling adult. He pulls himself to his feet on any adult body that is willing to support him and he joins the other crawlers to investigate the instruments basket.

The leader is happy for the children to join in or withdraw as they want.

When Niall likes a song, he joins in with the actions, and when he doesn't, he finds something else to do. The leader of this group of about eight children tunes in to each child and has begun to notice how each of them communicates their likes and dislikes. As Niall initiates clapping, she starts to sing the clapping song.

I have noticed how each child participates, secure with their carer and the space and freedom to move and explore. I have noted how they enjoy the repetition of the familiar songs and signs – songs which are relevant to them, about bath time, getting dressed and the actions for communication.

I have also noticed that the carers, the other mothers and I, are getting to know each other's children and how they communicate, what causes them stress and anxiety, and how they like to be handled and responded to. It is wonderful to experience group care in this way. I remember how this felt for me when my own children were young and I met with friends regularly, whether it was informally in our homes or when I was part of a toddler group.

I don't remember this being my experience in church crèches, as we always seemed to be with different people on a rota.

Babies have a magnetic pull to get others to pay them attention. They then let you know if they want to communicate with you – often looking at their primary carer to check with emotional response, looking for assurance that all is OK. This is called social referencing, checking their safety with their secure carer before pursuing a new relationship or conversation. The baby is using their reading of facial expressions as their source of information about what to do next. This is an important time for the baby to begin to extend their world safely.

Around this time, often about eight to nine months, the baby is also becoming aware that they are a separate being from their primary carer and is beginning to become unhappy at being left. This is called separation anxiety. Again, this is a normal aspect of social and emotional development, and the baby needs plenty of reassurance and a settling-in period. This period needs to be led by the parent and baby – both need time to adjust to separation. Some parents will need to stay for several weeks; others may only stay one week.

It is suggested that our later social intelligence is particularly responsive to the experiences we go through between the ages of six to eighteen months.[2] It is a time when the infant is still organizing experiences and is unable to predict events in the way that they will be able to do when they grow older. In reality, this is often the time when infants are experiencing multiple transitions.

In the past we have believed that because the child is young, they will not be affected by this. We need to take note of current research and adjust our thinking and expectations of young infants and their parents.

However, studying faces is a powerful way of adding to the connections in the brain, encouraging the brain to grow more. When the baby first smiles they are imitating the facial expressions they have observed. The response of others to a smile is so rewarding that the baby connects this action with pleasure and repeats it! Each smile and positive look of pleasure raises the heart rate in the infant and produces beta-endorphins which are released into the circulation. These are natural opioids which make us feel better! It is also thought that they assist in helping neurons to develop by regulating glucose and insulin.[3] Dopamine is also produced, which helps brain tissue to grow.

Therefore, all in all, feeling pleasure is good for the infant – and it is good for all of us throughout life!

So what about stress?

Stress is such a common term in our culture. You can go on stress management courses, read self-help books or have therapy. It is calculated that nearly 10 million working days are lost each year due to stress[4] and many of us carry stress in our bodies with bad backs, exhaustion and burnout.

Why?

Of course, there are many reasons, societal and personal, and I don't intend to consider those here. Stress is the state of high arousal – when all our senses are heightened and we are trying hard to regulate our emotions, with limited success. The response to stress is managed by chemical reactions which are linked to the hypothalamus in the brain. This part of the brain produces cortisol, which is a hormone. Scientific studies suggest that cortisol levels are raised when we wake in the morning, helping to provide us with energy for the day; they then decrease in the evening when we are going to sleep. Cortisol, along with other hormones, helps to regulate our emotional state. The brain responds to stressful experiences by creating more cortisol to help the person deal with the situation.

The human baby is more dependent on others at birth than any animal baby. The baby depends on its carers to manage stressful experiences and situations for them, as they have very low levels of cortisol at birth. This means that they can become very distressed if there is no one to respond to their anxiety, through touch, the human voice and familiar smells. As the baby begins to establish their own routine, the cortisol levels begin to take the pattern for adult life, but Gerhardt[5] comments that it is not until a child is about four years old that this pattern is established.

There are many different views on how to respond to a crying infant.

Personally, I think that if a child is upset, there is a reason, and my task is to comfort the child and find out what the reason is – and then respond to this. I do not believe that it is helpful to suggest that a child is "just putting it on" or "will get over it". Cortisol is a vital hormone, helping us to manage our stressful emotions, and we all need a certain level of stress. However, too much stress over a sustained period of time causes the child to remain in a heightened state of anxiety with a heightened level of cortisol. This is harmful and may affect the child's response levels to stress later in life and the way that they develop strategies to cope.

So, what am I suggesting?

Let's go back to the concept of "tuning in" to the child. By this I mean using all our skills in order to listen, read, hear and respond to the 100 languages of children. We need to give time to find out how the child is feeling and to respond with affection, love and comfort – as well as enthusiasm, delight and laughter. We need to avoid our natural default position of assuming that we know what the child needs, feels or wants.

All children, but particularly children under three years of age, need to feel secure. In British society we are very conscious of the need to safeguard children and therefore all people involved with children will have a CRB (Criminal Records Bureau) check, all groups will register who is with them and will conform to the ratio of children to adults for the specific age, and many crèches will give children labels to wear on their backs.

But what about *emotional* security?

God has made us as relational beings. We cannot exist healthily in isolation and all of us get to know about God's love through the way that people respond to us.

How do we respond to the following concerns for the very young child?

- Let me feel that you care.
- Do you know my world, and the people and places that are special to me?
- Are you hearing me?
- Am I involved in your plans?
- Do I know about God and his love through the way you care for me and the relationship we share?

Here are some possible strategies to provide for the social and emotional needs of children under 3 years

- What about a system to record each child's particular information and interests? Perhaps this could be a simple cardex system noting each child's personal information, including names of the family, specific key words, sleep routines, ways of being comforted and the names of other adults and carers, so that you can respond sensitively to each child. This information will need to be kept in a locked cabinet when not in use to protect the confidentiality of all children and their families. Families will need to give their consent for this information to be kept.

- Make sure that there is time when children are being settled in each session to find out any particular information from the parent/carer that may affect the child. A bad night's sleep, the cat going missing, an argument with a sibling – even seemingly insignificant things can affect the way a child feels about being with others and separated from family.

- What about the feelings of the parent? I can remember feeling very anxious at times about leaving my children in some groups. Sometimes it was due to things we as a family were facing, but at other times I sensed the tension or unpreparedness or lack of empathy for children in the group they were about to attend. Inevitably, my children also sensed my tension and I needed reassurance before I could give them reassurance. Unfortunately, I am one of those people who are not very good at making my needs known verbally, and I hope that people will read me. There are others like me who are still learning to communicate their feelings, and leaders of children's groups need to be able to "tune in" to adults too.

- It is so important to have consistency of carers for children in group care. This can be very difficult for churches to manage. Some churches are very large and need to consider the size of their groups as well as the accommodation and people to run the groups. Other churches may be very small with a more transient congregation and few people to help. Whatever the context, consistency is really vital for these children under three. There needs to be familiarity, a sense of belonging and a genuine welcome. Children need people who know them, understand them and will be there for them. You need to think how you will organize the team to provide the greatest possible consistency and continuity for the children.

- We need to be astute observers. This will be so much easier if we are able to spend time regularly with the children. We need to observe the children's body language, actions, relationships with others, and their emerging language. We also need to learn how to interpret these observations so that they are not based on our assumptions of what we think the child is telling us, but instead we are trying genuinely to understand what the child is trying to convey to us. This will help us to know how to make meaningful connections with each individual child. Some children need time to come to you; others will want an instant hug. Some children will take a while to settle and may need a familiar person to do a familiar action with them before they are able to settle into the different environment.

One day, as I dropped Evie off at nursery, she clung to me, even though I stayed to play for some time; she was distressed at the thought of my leaving. It was her mum's first day back at work, life was changing for her and she was anxious. After a while, her key worker suggested that they go together to check on the nursery rabbit. He knew that she loved this rabbit and this was a treat, so I handed over a distraught Evie, knowing that she would settle now. Both her key worker and I have been observing what helps her to work through her anxiety and cope with the situation.

- Church leaders should make sure that the adults working with children are emotionally intelligent themselves. The adults need the time and resources to be trained, so that they know about the development of the young child, about Children's Rights and current thinking and research about children's learning and care. It is important that there are shared beliefs about the purpose of children's church and the view of children, so that they are consistent. It is valuable for a team to have time to reflect together on their practice and relationships. This sounds like a tall order, but we have similar expectations of our church leaders regarding their leadership of adults.

- Children are very sensitive spiritually. It is my belief that the way we care for children and respond to them respectfully as strong, competent, knowledgeable and sensitive people will influence the way that they think about God. Of course, they may grow up to have no conscious memories of their time in crèche or children's church under the age of three, but they will have registered what it felt like and will have made connections with this place called church.

But what about the parents and the people in church who are willing to care for these very young children in children's church or crèche?

Care of the very youngest children is a big responsibility, often overlooked by others. When we work with young children we are always also working with their families – we cannot separate our pastoral care. I think that it is important that we offer supervision and/or mentoring to leaders – giving them the opportunity to off-load difficult concerns within a confidential environment. Although we have given examples of children throughout this book, we have made sure that children's and adults' identities are confidential, unless we have explicit permission to name them. As with all work with children and their families, attention to ethical issues is a must.

Other leaders and people in the church need to recognize the responsibility of looking after young children, and you may want them to read this book to understand why.

St Ignatius of Loyola, the founder of the Society of Jesus (the Jesuits), is alleged to have said: "Give me the child till the age of seven and I will show you the man."

As we work with young children, we are their role models, and we need to be positive ones. Young children pick up on all we do and say and will weigh this up against the messages we want to convey to them. They cannot and do not distinguish between the intended message and the hidden message. Hidden messages are those actions and gestures that we do subconsciously or intending that children don't notice. For example, if we are asked by another person to do something we don't want to do and when their back is turned, we raise our eyes and pull a face, what message will the children get?

However, I am always comforted by these words from Isaiah 40:11, where the prophet is speaking about God's leadership:

> *He [God] tends his flock like a shepherd: He gathers the lambs in his arms and carries them close to his heart; he gently leads those that have young.*

Listen to the tenderness and gentleness in this scenario. Where is the stress, the rush, the pressure to "convert" children? What are the relationships like? Take time to get to know individual children.

Max De Pree writes of his thoughts and feelings as he "stepped" into the role of father for his premature granddaughter Zoe, who was born at twenty-four weeks:

> Until now I have been spoiled by having four children and seven grandchildren born without problems – "only normal".
>
> You feel weightless and fragile. How mystical to hold you in my hands. Your eyes seem to search for me. Your forehead wrinkles. You feel like a tiny, tentative person – a fledgling.
>
> How many have ever experienced touching life that ought not yet to be out of the womb! Your tubes and monitors reinforce the sense of how close you are each moment to eternity. I am holding you on the edge of everlasting life, which is so obviously more substantial than you feel to me. I surely can't explain it, but you feel to me like a breath of God. One of these exquisite feelings one cannot describe. You in all your innocent, complicated existence must be closer to God than the rest of us, and holding you brings us closer to him. No wonder Jesus tells us to be like a child if we want to enter the kingdom of heaven. Surely reality is spiritual.[6]

So relationships are critical for a young child's healthy development. But they are also important for us too. When we "tune in" to the young child and are connecting with them, chemicals are released in our bodies too which make us feel good. We are wonderfully designed and put together so that our social, emotional and spiritual health is sustained by positive, trusting relationships.

Reflection

- How do you and others in your team prepare yourselves emotionally to work with children under three years old?

- How do you make sure that your environment for the youngest children is an emotionally safe place?

- How are these children learning about God through you?

  - *Is it reciprocal?*

CHAPTER 8

Play Time

Are my senses stimulated?

Isobel

> I am writing this chapter from Cornwall, staying in a farm building overlooking the Camel estuary. It is late October, and the weather is sunny, windy and very autumnal. Yesterday I went for a walk down the country lanes towards the sea. All of my senses were stimulated as I ate the late blackberries from the hedgerows, was buffeted by the wind, heard the cows, the occasional car and the birds, smelled the sea air and the farm smells, looked out over the landscape and gazed at the rolling clouds, and engaged totally with my surroundings as I slipped in the mud while trying to take a short cut over the rocks at low tide!
>
> The previous night I had arrived in Cornwall with friends. I was unwell, exhausted and uninspired. A good sleep, time, space and the freedom to pace my day, plus the beautiful natural environment, gave me fresh energy and a new perspective.

So what is it that has made the difference?

First, the generosity of the friends I am with. Sharing their space with me, trusting me, loving me and being interested in me. This sense of being wanted, accepted, understood and welcomed is a vital aspect of the environment for children.

My friends not only allow me, but also expect me to help myself to food, activities and the resources within their cottage. They want me to feel that I have an equal place here – a sense of shared ownership. This sense of ownership is also important when providing an environment for the youngest children.

The Cornish countryside, with its open space, access to the natural world and the stimulation of all of my senses, enables me to think big, connect with the Creator of this world and explore and discover the area for myself.

Think back to a place where you are able to find space, time and inspiration.

What is it like?

What makes it a special place?

Where do your youngest children go in your church?

Perhaps there is a space where babies and parents can go if their child is wriggly, or a crèche in another room, or different groups for babies, toddlers and pre-school children. Wherever it is and whatever the age range, the environment will speak volumes to the children and their families.

By "environment" I mean the people, the physical space and the atmosphere.

In northern Italy, in the region of Reggio Emilia, there are a number of nurseries for young children which follow what is now known as the Reggio Emilia approach. Their underlying philosophy is that they see the child as strong, competent and knowledgeable.

The nurseries were set up after the Second World War. A group of mothers were so concerned about the devastating destruction of family unity in the region caused by allegiance to different sides of the conflict that they wanted to educate children in such a way that this would never happen again. Loris Malaguzzi, an educator, worked with them to establish nurseries that were set within the wider community, where the children would be seen as equal members of the community, and where the community was involved in the nurseries.

Staff are seen as co-researchers with the children, so that children and adults explore, investigate and discover things together – a genuine reciprocity for learning and building relationships. The atmosphere that is created by the adults in the room will have a big effect on the children and their families as they arrive. Reflect on this quote and feel the emotional pressure.

> *Waterloo station was crowded.*
> *But more than the crowding of people was the crowding of anxiety* *and stress…*[1]

Thinking about the environment, preparing for the session and having time to reflect together as a group will help to create a calm ambience. Any anxiety and stress carried by the adults will be passed on to the children and their families and will create a stressful atmosphere. Praying together and asking a small group of people to be a prayer support group can make a difference.

Remember, children are brilliant sensors, but poor interpreters of the reasons behind an atmosphere.

The choice of people to lead the groups is very important.

> In one nursery I visit regularly, there is one adult who is a magnet for all the children. She is more than the Pied Piper as she doesn't lead the children from the front; the children are equals with her; there is no power contest. As she enters the room, the children rush towards her – these children are two to three years old. She knows them and they know her. She listens to their individual ways of communicating with her and each child in the group is acknowledged and is a participant of the group.

What is it about this person?

She clearly loves being with children and sees them as interesting and engaging people. She is not patronizing, she shows real empathy and is never dismissive of a child's feelings. She respects and values children as unique, intelligent individuals. This is demonstrated by her genuine interest in their interests and discoveries. She also recognizes the importance of the group and supports the group dynamic.

What are your expectations of the children? Do you want the children to:

> *grow up as competent and confident learners and communicators,*
> *healthy in mind, body and spirit, secure in their sense of belonging and*
> *in the knowledge that they make a valued contribution to society.*[2]

What about the physical environment?

In the Reggio Emilia approach, the environment is known as "the third teacher", recognizing what a powerful impact it has on children and their attitude towards learning.

> Sometimes when I am teaching my students, I change the layout of the classroom and set it up as an examination room. The tables are all in rows and spaced out so that each person is isolated. I place a piece of blank paper and a pen on each table and then I set up the whiteboard and my desk as I

would do any other week for my usual teaching sessions. I then leave the room and don't return until the dot of 9.00 a.m. (or whatever time the class should start). Without exception, the students sit down in the places provided, either talking in hushed tones or silent, always looking very anxious. Despite seeing my usual PowerPoint set-up and all my resources on the table, they immediately pick up the message of the environment and await "the exam".

You can imagine that this provokes a very lively debate about the impact of environments on our emotional, social and cognitive feelings. How we *feel* in any environment will influence our ability to relax, feel safe and secure, and feel OK about learning.

I believe that the environment is really critical when we want to engage children's spirituality. The whole concept of spirituality is complex and is discussed in depth by Rebecca Nye in her interesting book, *Children's Spirituality: What it is and why it matters.*[3]

There was a time, a few years ago, when the phrase "awe and wonder" was used within early years education to indicate the importance of encouraging children's spiritual development. Educators were encouraged to provide children with experiences that would arouse their sense of awe and wonder.

Natural light, adequate warmth, natural materials, a large mirror, space to move, soft comfy places to curl up, places to be out of sight – all these add to making an inviting environment for children and their families.

Reflect on this poem by William Henry Davies[4] and feel it as well as using your imagination and memory:

> ### Leisure
> *What is life if, full of care,*
> *We have no time to stand and stare.*
> *No time to stand beneath the boughs*
> *And stare as long as sheep and cows.*
> *No time to see, when woods we pass,*
> *Where squirrels hide their nuts in grass.*
> *No time to see in broad daylight,*
> *Streams full of stars, like skies at night.*
> *No time to turn at Beauty's glance,*
> *And watch her feet, how they can dance.*

No time to wait till her mouth can
Enrich that smile her eyes began.
A poor life this, if full of care,
We have no time to stand and stare.

I know that churches are sometimes very restricted by the spaces they have to accommodate different groups, but why do the adults usually have the best space? If you were to look at your church accounts and budget over the last few years, is the spending on improving environments equal across the age ranges?

If not, why not?

Whatever the accommodation you have for the children from birth to three years, something can be done to improve it, or perhaps you will need to negotiate a swap with other groups.

It is suggested that St Jerome said: "Apparently small details should not be ignored, for it is only through them that these designs are possible"

And it is the small details that can make such a difference.

Gandini,[5] writing about the ethos of environments within Reggio Emilia, states: "We think that the space has to be a sort of aquarium that mirrors the ideas, values, attitudes and cultures of the people who live in it."

So, look at the area set aside for children. What is the entrance like?

Look carefully at what is on the walls. Are the images and posters appropriate for *this* group of children and their families? Do they reflect their lives and cultures? All too often we associate Disney with young children and cover walls with pictures we assume will interest them. How can we create a sense of awe and wonder?

Depending on the space available, hangings and mobiles help to soften the environment and can provide slowly moving objects for babies to watch. Old CDs make great reflective mobiles and anything that will catch and reflect the light will bring the magic of moving light into the area. A large mirror offers lots of experiences for the developing child, from seeing a reflection of "another" to recognizing their own reflection. Places like IKEA sell drapes which can easily be set up and put away quickly. Even cheaper are Scrapstores, which sell excess materials from shops and factories for a minimal price. Try to find your nearest store and you will never be short of fascinating materials!

Children in the Way?

A friend of mine is involved in a project which provides creative resources to provoke and inspire children's imaginations and creativity in schools and nurseries. She talks of setting up "fascination traps". By this she means providing resources which will arouse children's interests and present them with opportunities for exploration and investigation.

How do you set up fascination traps for the children from birth to three years? Consider this quote (from *Walley's Stories* by Vivian Gussin Paley) and reflect on the kinds of materials and equipment you have for your group:

> *Every day young children are behaving like architects, astronauts, authors, builders, designers, drivers, initiators, inventors, originators, pilots, mathematicians, musicians, scientists... and so on. Young thinkers construct some wonderful and apparently bizarre reasons for why things happen, when drawing on their present knowledge to create explanations which are logical to them at that time.[6]*

So what equipment, resources and materials are available for the children? I would argue that quality is more important than quantity and open-ended resources are more interesting and have a longer interest span than one-use objects. Stacking cups and building blocks offer a variety of possibilities, whereas while a fixed pop-up toy may provide interest and a diversion, it doesn't stimulate the imagination. A box of donated toys may be better taken to a charity shop than added to the crèche!

I have always preferred the use of natural materials in the production of toys. For me, they are more soothing and relaxing to touch and have connections with the natural, created world – which very young children are already exploring. However, there are many interesting man-made resources which are often preferred by adults as they are seen as hygienic, more colourful and visually stimulating.

But we need to think about stimulating all the senses in our spaces for children from birth to three years.

When Evie was about five months old and ready to sit supported with cushions, I had great fun putting together a treasure basket for her. I found a simple but safe basket and filled it with wooden objects such as a dolly peg, a honey spoon, a wooden block and a wooden spoon. I added objects made of metal and a natural sponge, among other items.

I think her parents were rather sceptical about this rather dull-looking basket. She already had a selection of beautiful toys. However, as time went on, they noticed how Evie would select an item and explore it for its taste, texture, smell, feel and sound. This basket interested her for several months, long after she became mobile.

Treasure baskets were introduced by Elinor Goldshmied[7] and there is information about them on the internet. It is well worth investigating and they are so much cheaper and more enduring than manufactured toys.

It is important that the basket is well made and fairly sturdy. Fill the basket with a variety of objects such as the ones listed above, keys, a bath-plug on a chain, a rubber door-wedge, wooden toys, different natural fabrics, lavender bags and all things sensory. Never leave the infant unsupervised but do ensure that there are cushions to prop up the child and a clear space without other distractions. More than one infant can explore the basket – it is interesting to watch how babies observe each other and play alongside. Sometimes they imitate each other, sometimes they both want what the other has and sometimes they are self-absorbed. Whatever else is happening, they are learning about the world through their senses.

Every crèche with children who are beginning to sit should have a variety of treasure baskets which can be given to a child to explore. As long as adults have checked them for safety and hygiene, the adult should not need to intervene but should allow the child time to explore at their own pace.

Whatever the age of the child under three years, the selection of resources for children needs to be thought through carefully, resisting the temptation to tip out the regular box of toys or set out things on tables in the same way each week. It is important to think about "intelligent materials". As Guidici and Rinaldi comment:

> If we value children's desire and pleasure in carrying out
> investigations, either by themselves or in groups, then we must make
> sure that the sort of materials we provide allow this to happen.[8]

When the room is set up for children, can they select materials and resources for themselves?

All too often the temptation is to get things out, leaving little room for choice and decision making. Supporting independence and encouraging a child's participation in their play and activity is an important element of respectful relationships, one in which our view of the child is can-do rather than can't-do. Freely chosen resources also give the child the opportunity to use something that interests them. Starting from what children already know and allowing them to pursue their own interests is not only recognized as good practice in early years education and care, but it makes it easier for them to learn.

It is also important to ensure that young children have time to think, explore and become involved in an activity.

Knowing each child well will ensure that activities and resources are interesting to the children and are sufficiently challenging but not unreachable. The education system in England has been a "top-down" approach. Poor results at sixteen years mean more pressure to teach children to learn their phonics at a younger age. Evidence from Europe indicates that early formal learning does not produce better results later. It suggests that the converse is true. Young children need time and space to become skilful tool-users, know about the different textures of dry and wet sand, water, paint and soil, have control of their large and small motor skills, and be proficient communicators, before they are expected to sit and write or draw!

One of the unfortunate side-effects of studies of the brain and the importance of stimulation for babies is the anxiety felt by some parents that their child is not stimulated enough. This can lead to "hot-housing" children and buying flash cards and other resources to speed up their learning. One curriculum publication comments:

> Gardeners don't plant runner beans in January to get an earlier harvest than their neighbours; if they tried, they would probably get shrivelled and stunted beans. They fertilise the ground in the early months of the year, so that when the beans are planted – at the right time – they will flourish.[9]

So, the environment for the youngest children needs to be sensory, stimulating, secure and appealing. Each church context will make decisions about the age range for a crèche, what to do with two year olds, and whether the three year olds will be with older or younger children. There needs to be space for sleep, for changing nappies and for routine care needs. All this has to be thought through as a team, with an agreed protocol about responding to individual children's routines.

Whatever the decisions, the crèche needs to be planned as carefully as any other group in the church. Having a budget each year, however small, will enable planned purchasing of resources. Asking people with creative gifts to come and help plan the physical environment to ensure that there are interesting hangings, fabrics, mobiles and comfortable areas for children and adults, will ease the stress of knowing where to start. Crèches can become noisy places and often are in echoing buildings. Sometimes people use background music to provide a calm environment. Perhaps this is calming for the adult, but for the young child who is learning to talk and discriminate sounds, background music creates a confusion of sounds.

Going back to my experiences of Sing and Sign sessions, even the youngest baby will enjoy singing and actions, and a short time together as a group with singing, instruments and rhymes is a valuable experience for children in crèche – particularly if there is repetition and action. Shakers are always a great hit – and adults enjoy the activity too.

As the toddler becomes more agile and articulate, they will enjoy stories and activities – but their sitting-still limit is very short. Children are designed to be physically active and have a natural rhythm that includes times of high activity and moments of quiet and reflection.

Stories are very powerful ways for a young child to learn about God, but the stories must be meaningful and pertinent. While I think that it is a great experience for both adult and young child to share a book together, I am a great believer in telling stories using facial expressions, vocal tone, volume and pace and some well-chosen props. This method frees up the child's imagination and allows the senses to engage with the story. It also means that children are not scrabbling over each other to try to see the pictures.

Having told the story, I would leave the props for children to play with and encourage them to play with whatever resources I have available. Ideally this would always include sand, water and the outside space. Children are then free to re-enact the story, create their own stories, explore their own ideas or just be.

This gives the adults time to spend with the children playing alongside them if this is what the child wants, chatting with them or providing additional resources. If the families have given you permission, you can capture the child's significant moments on camera and share this with their families later. Digital cameras are a great invention and can provide evidence of the processes children go through in their play. These photos, along with any artefacts the child produces, can enable the parents and children to share more about their session together when they go home. You can also use the photographs to document your group on the walls of the room you are in. However, you will need to be very careful about ethical issues and must take the photos down at the end of each session if the room is a multi-purpose one.

Consider the following questions as you reflect on your own provision for children from birth to three years:

- What do the youngest children of the early twenty-first century need from their experiences of church?
- What sorts of things might be good for them?
- What kinds of adults might be best fitted to work with them?
- What might their planned experiences be like?
- What kinds of environments would be best suited to their needs and the ways in which they spend their time?[10]

Socrates is credited with saying: "Wisdom begins with wonder." And Barbara Hepworth, the sculptor, said: "Perhaps what one wants to say is formed in childhood and the rest of one's life is spent trying to say it."

In conclusion to this chapter, I return to my thoughts at the beginning: to ponder on the amazing beauty of the natural world. If God has created such an incredible world for us to live in, and has made us in his image, then surely, as children explore their own creativity and imagination, it must open up connections between the Creator and the created, and release a sense of awe and wonder.

Reflection

- What does your environment look like from a baby's or toddler's perspective when on the floor?
- What does your environment "feel" like?
- What are children and their families learning about God through the environment?
- What works well in this environment for babies and toddlers?
- What do I need to change?

CHAPTER 9

Timed to Perfection

What a mess!

Isobel

I remember when my children were young, they loved a television programme called *Bric-a-brac*. I hated it, and used to grit my teeth as I watched it with them.

Why?

The set was such a mess. There was stuff everywhere and the presenter was always rummaging through the shelves and cupboards to find the materials he needed to make whatever his project was for that week. I hated the clutter; my children loved the energy and enthusiasm of the presenter and his wonderful creative ideas.

And my children now?

They are all very creative and imaginative, and are willing to have a go at anything. Fortunately, I didn't let my dislike of clutter stop their exploration of materials, their creation of models and their inquiries into how things worked – which usually involved taking them apart!

> I also remember a friend calling to visit after the birth of my second child. She was a health visitor and turned up unannounced. I apologized for the mess in the living room. As usual, my toddler had turned out the toy cupboard and we probably had playdough out as well. Celia told me in no uncertain terms that had the place been immaculate, she would have been concerned about the well-being of my two small children. This was an important lesson for me. As a teacher, I would expect there to be a mess after having paint, sand, water, playdough and other materials out, but I needed to be reminded that this was true in the home too – albeit, with different materials.

I sometimes think that churches need to be reminded of this.

Children in the Way?

Perhaps it goes back to the discourse or belief that the church holds about children; maybe it is the type of teaching materials that the church has been using over the years; possibly it is the need of the adults to be in control in a structured environment that prevents the opportunity for play with natural materials that may make a mess.

To return to the findings from brain studies, researchers now suggest that babies are born with an innate curiosity and a desire to investigate and explore. They also point out that babies can get bored and need interesting environments as well as companionship and stimulation. Play with natural materials provides countless opportunities for these young scientists and will help children to make sense of their world and make connections with other aspects of learning and relationships.

Purposeful play is the way that children learn.

What is the difference between play and purposeful play?

It is sometimes argued that play that is not purposeful is merely being occupied rather than being involved with play. Play theorists suggest that play is self-chosen and may be solitary or may be with others. Freely chosen play allows a child to make choices and decisions. This will give them the opportunities to solve problems, test hypotheses, create new worlds, re-enact existing ones, face difficult emotions, attempt to understand experiences and build relationships. Children also use play to explore language and develop their communication skills. They will make marks and start to "write", become expert mathematicians and run a business!

Lev Vygotsky, a Russian psychologist, whose work is highly regarded in education, suggests that a child is a head taller than themselves when they are playing. In other words, their abilities are heightened through play.

Evie was on her mobile phone one morning. It was an old phone which she had initially rejected because it was broken, but over time she took to phoning her friends. Aged twenty-one months, the conversation went like this:

"Hello, Grandad. You OK? Good. At home? Good. In Bristol? Ahh, Good."

This was repeated several times, phoning Mummy, Niall and Gla-gla with the phone propped between her ear and shoulder, and doing something with her bag. She looked and sounded just like her mum on the phone; her tone, facial expressions and body language had been accurately observed and recorded and were being rehearsed.

One day I played alongside a little boy aged two with very little spoken language; he put a book in my hands, indicating that he wanted to share the book with me. We looked at the book, which I personally found rather dull. There were very few words and the pictures were uninspiring, until I turned a page and there was a digger. The body language of this child changed completely. His interest and imagination was clearly stimulated. We looked at the digger, talked about the digger, made the noises of the digger and then I spotted an orange toy digger on the window sill. With the book still open, this little boy played for a long time with his toy. He shovelled up pieces of construction and tipped them out in a pile. Back and forwards. He knew exactly what a digger does.

The following week, as he arrived in the nursery, he noticed me again. Taking the "digger" book from the book box, he brought it over to me and made the sounds and actions of the digger. We found the toy again and he returned to the activity from the previous week.

I commented earlier in the book that the structure of *Sesame Street*, the American TV programme for children, made a strong impression on me. I believe that children are making connections between their home lives, their community lives, their church lives and themselves all the time. As they participate in a story and songs which engage with their senses, so they will make further connections through their play. Adults do not need to direct the overall programme of a session for the youngest children, but they do need to plan carefully and provide rich, diverse materials, resources and equipment.

One of the important qualities of play that is often overlooked is that it is more concerned with the *process* than the final product.

I remember going to visit one of my childcare students one December day. They were making Christmas cards for the parents. I say "they" because it was really the adults who were making them. "They" had cut out red candles, green holly and a gold flame. I watched, horrified, as the adult "helped" the child to glue the candle with a glue stick, then together they placed the candle onto the card, and the adult encouraged the child to put pressure on it so that it would stick. The adult's hand hovered close, ready to pounce if the candle slipped out of place. This action was repeated with the holly and flame until the adult said to the child, "Won't Mummy be pleased with the card you have made?"

Children in the Way?

Who designed it, prepared it and made it? Not the child, for certain.

How can you feel confident in your achievements when someone else won't trust you to be creative yourself?

Why are we concerned about providing activities with an end product?

Are we afraid that the parents won't know what we have been doing?

Are we worried that the children will forget the "theme" for that week?

Are we anxious that we won't know how to fill the time if we don't have planned and prepared craft activity?

Is it what we have always done?

Play is so often thought of as the thing that children do when they are not learning, but nothing could be further from the truth.

Through play, children are making sense of their world and developing the confidence to be learners and to learn how to learn.

Young children also need time.

Time to do things for themselves.

> My granddaughter loves to do things independently and get dressed on her own. One morning we were both getting dressed together and were running late for nursery. I suggested that we had a race to see who would be first. What a stupid suggestion! Putting on tights and doing up a cardigan are complicated tasks. It took time and I had to resist the temptation to help her, just to speed things up. She knew what to do, she knew how to do it, and she just needed the time to do it for herself. And what a sense of achievement she felt!

I recently heard about the four states from incompetence to competence. We start in a state of unconscious incompetence, when we don't know that we can't do something. We then move into the state of conscious incompetence, when we know we can't do something. The next state is conscious competence, when we know we can do something but have to concentrate hard on it, before finally becoming unconsciously competent, when we do things without thinking. My granddaughter was operating in conscious competence, which is the optimum place for learning.

It is rather like me learning to ride a bike!

As a nine year old I watched my brother on his bike. It looked so easy and I *knew* that I could do it. My dad bought me a second-hand bike and I sat on it at the top of the drive, wobbled down the hill, crashed into the wall at the bottom and damaged my bike and myself. I was moving from a state of unconscious incompetence to conscious incompetence. As I became more skilful, I became confident and competent as a cyclist, and I knew it. Now as an adult, I am plucking up the courage to cycle to work through the traffic. Last year I felt sure I could do it. Now I am sure I can't, but hopefully by the time you read this I will be confident and competent and conscious!

Planning a session for young children (ages: from birth to three years)

Your provision for the youngest children will inevitably depend on the size of your church and the buildings. If you have many children in your church, you may well have an under pre-school group and a pre-school group.

If possible, it is best to have two areas for the under threes, so that one area can be quiet, with comfortable seating for parents and privacy for breast-feeding mothers and sleeping babies. The other area can be for more mobile children, with opportunities for physical play, creative activities, singing and stories.

Even better, access to an outdoor area means that children can play and babies can sleep in the fresh air. However, this needs to be checked for safety before the children arrive and supervised appropriately, maintaining the regulation ratios for children of this age.

I think that crèche needs to be planned and prayed about in the same way that any other group in the church is.

Resources need to be selected carefully

Open-ended materials encourage creative play; puzzles need to have enough space to be completed and kept for the duration of the session if the child wants; books need to be carefully selected and should include non-stereotypical, positive images; and all toys need to be clean and in good repair.

Sensory materials, which engage all the senses and encourage active, investigative and creative expressions, are appropriate for very young children.

Although there will be a different mix of children each week, those in charge of the crèche need to get to know the children and their families. This will help in the planning for the session. Some questions that they could consider are:

- Is the train track popular at the moment?
- Are children enjoying the stacking blocks?
- Which books are in demand?

Remember that less is more and space to move is essential.

We often make the mistake of putting out too much. It is better to have boxes or baskets with resources available if needed, rather than putting everything out at once.

Planning for singing and stories

Who will tell or read the story? Do you need props? What about using a Story Sack? You can buy ready-made sacks but you can also make these very cheaply. I have often collected items from home such as a baby's bottle, baby clothes and so on for the story of Moses as a baby; or a picnic basket with rolls and small fish for the story of Jesus feeding the 5,000. I have used a variety of boxes, baskets, bags and cases – all containers which the smallest children love to put things in and take things out of.

> On one occasion I was telling the story of Moses with a group of two to three year olds and decided to create a simple Story Sack. I knew that some of them either had or were expecting a new sibling. I filled a Moses basket with items for a baby including a baby doll. As I told the story, I produced different items and the children enjoyed telling what they were and how to use them. We dressed the baby and fed it as I continued with the story. "Baby Moses" was put into the basket and we took him to the river and watched out for him as I continued to tell them about the princess arriving and his mother coming to look after him. They then played with the doll and the props.

This story was meaningful for these children because they knew about babies coming and they understood the process we went through in the story. The vocabulary I used was familiar and repetitive, so they could join in and memorize it.

Even the young children will love a short, active story. The props can then be left out so that children can re-enact the story if they wish. I have watched children who are still learning to talk, act out a story with props – using their imaginations and creating their own stories.

My granddaughter is two and a half years old and she loves stories. For several months now we have made up stories together and each time we meet she says, "Tell me about a story." Recently, as she was getting ready for bed and her parents were in her room with her, she sat on a small chair and declared to them, "I am a story maker."

Her mother replied, "You mean you are a story teller."

"Yes," said my granddaughter, "I am a story *maker*," and she picked up a book and started to make up a story from the pictures. She was imaginative, articulate and interesting – and not yet three years old.

Songs and rhymes are brilliant ways to support language development and young children have great memories – far better than mine! Repetition, actions and movement reinforce the language and most children will enjoy joining in.

Instruments such as shakers and bells are always popular.

At "Sing and Sign" a box of instruments is used. The babies know the routine of the session and the teachers' rule that you have to sit with your carer before you get an instrument – and they do! Niall is always quick to return to me and always selects an orange shaker.

So, what about your weekly routine?

Even in crèche, the routine is very important. This is the way that babies and young children orient their day. With a regular routine they can predict what will happen next and feel more secure.

Adults working in the crèche that week will also know what to expect and how to engage with the children.

What about the practical needs of the children?

Food, drink during the session, bottles for babies, nappy changing, potty training, using the toilet – there are many things that you will need to decide as a team in consultation with parents and your Child Protection officer. So often, it is these practical details that can cause the tensions and difficulties within groups for very young children.

What about boundaries?

Young children need to know what the boundaries are and these need to be consistent. We have boundaries to ensure that the children are safe, yet have lots of freedom within the boundaries to make choices and have control of their lives, as is appropriate for them. It is said that boundaries without relationship lead to rebellion, so positive relationships with children are critical; and boundaries plus relationship lead to security; and relationship without boundaries leads to insecurity.

A typical crèche session

- Setting up the area based on the pre-prepared plans, and time to exchange information with the key members of the team.

- Start with signing children in, exchanging information with parents and settling children in to play in the prepared environment.

- Freely chosen play with all the adults engaged with the babies and children.

- A brief story, singing and movement time.

- Freely chosen play – some older children may be interested in an activity which is related to the story, but no pressure!

- Pick-up time. This time can become quite difficult for young children and we need to remember that it is another transition time for them. If it is possible, it is good to warn them a few minutes before their parents arrive.

- Debrief time and noting down any particular concerns, things that have worked well or resources that need to be included next week. If there is a different leader next week, what about having a crèche noticeboard area and leaving planning ideas there?

Points to remember for the crèche team

- Never talk about the children or their families within the hearing of children – however young. This is not only disrespectful, but it will convey powerful messages to the child.

- Don't use crèche time to catch up with friends but make sure that all adults are engaging with the children or babies, although there are times when children don't want adults to play. This is a time to watch and listen to their "hundred languages".

- Be sensitive to the child if they are misbehaving. Never shame a child or humiliate them in front of others. Sometimes, it is your own child who plays up when you are there. I remember this clearly but I don't think I always handled it well. I was too concerned about what other people thought about my parenting skills. Often, my children found it hard to share me with others when they were very young, and I needed to be more sensitive to their needs while still caring for the other children in the group. This is why ratios for adults to babies are so high. They need lots of attention.

- Sensitive handling of babies and young children: remember to tune in to them and read their cues about touch, personal space and volume of voice.

What are babies and very young children learning about God through their crèche groups? If they are cared for by playful adults who enjoy their company and are interested in them as people, what will this tell them about God?

Do we believe that God is interested in play, discovery and experimentation? Does he enjoy laughter and fun? Does he understand fear of separation?

The title of this chapter, "Timed to Perfection" is not about having a timetable for the group which is set in stone and inflexible. It is about the thinking and preparation that take place *beforehand* so that during the session you are able to be responsive to the needs of each child and their families, and give them time.

The subtitle of this chapter is "What a mess!" Why is it that we often equate young children with mess?

Is this a derogatory term?

My dictionary suggests that a mess is a dirty or untidy, chaotic or confused state.

Children in the Way?

Young children need to be able to explore and discover different materials, and we need to *avoid* considering their environment or activities as "messy" – otherwise we are passing on those hidden messages about the value of what they do and our respect for how they do it.

- What are the dropping-off and picking-up times like for children under three?

  - *How could you make these times less stressful for the children?*

- How do you plan the session for children under three?

What did you do at pre-school today?

'What did you do at pre-school today?'
'Well, I sat at the dough table and rolled the dough in my hands.
Lucy said hers was a snake but mine, mine was a worm.
The lady talked about long ones and short ones, and medium sized ones,
and Sarah rolled her dough so long it went right over the edge of the table.
And no one said "what are you going to make – a cake would be nice."'

'Yes, but then what did you do?'
'I played on the climbing frame
and, do you know Mummy,
I can climb to the very top step.'

'Yes, but did you do anything today?'
'Sarah and me went to the paint table.
It was lovely; all gooey and slippery on our hands,
and we made lots of patterns with our fingers and elbows.
Sarah had yellow paint and I had red
and Mummy, do you know what,
if you mix red paint and yellow paint together it goes ORANGE!
(And nobody said "what a mess you've made").'

'Yes, but what else have you done?'
'At milk time it was my turn
to pour the milk and give the apples out
and I didn't spill any.'

'And then did you do anything?'
'I made lovely traily patterns in the sand,
and Sarah and I had a race to see
who could put the sand in the sand wheel quickest.'

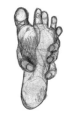

''But, then did you do anything?'
'At story time I was tired so I sat on the lady's lap
and the story was about a caterpillar
– and do you know what Mummy,
caterpillars turn into beautiful butterflies!'

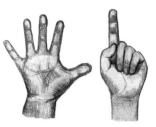

Children in the Way?

'So, did you do anything today?'
'We sang "Happy Birthday" to Nicholas
and counted the candles on his cake.'

'But, did you do anything today?'
'Yes, when the lady said it's time to tidy up,
I quickly painted you a picture
'cos I knew you'd say,

'What did you do at pre-school today?'

Sue Heard[1]

Section 4

Moving on Up!

This section will specifically address the age range of three to seven year olds by looking at issues that impact them at church. It will deal with the practicalities of building and running a team and how to lead the team to reflect on and then improve the quality for the children. It will tackle such concerns as conflict resolution in teams and how to support children in resolving their conflicts too. It will also deal with the very practical matters of resourcing children's church appropriately and planning a programme using the medium of story.

CHAPTER 10

Talking Time

Relationships matter

Carrie

Relationships with children

In my previous work of inspecting nurseries and observing students on teaching practice, I was able to observe the many different strategies people use to avoid "being present" with children. They include adults talking to adults, preparing food or materials or equipment, and looking busy without actually doing anything. I think this happens because focusing closely on children, whilst being immensely important, is also hard work, in that it demands our energy. If, for some reason, we are not at peace with ourselves – an unresolved upset at home, for instance – then we can be physically present with children but emotionally absent, because our focus is elsewhere as we are processing things internally. Therefore being present is not just a physical presence but also being emotionally available.

No wonder it is easier to be busy rather than listening.

Being completely available to children therefore means being at their physical level: sitting on their small chairs, sitting on the ground or kneeling so that our eyes are level with theirs. Then it means watching their body language and their actions, and listening to anything they say using words or sounds, remembering that they have a hundred languages, a hundred ways of communicating. At times it is important to watch and listen closely and wait to join in alongside them, maybe mirroring what they are playing with. At other times we need to respond to overtures made to us, and join in with their interests and preferences. Sometimes it may be important to ask a question or set a challenge that extends their thinking, rather than cutting across what they are doing. Joining in with what is taking up their attention and then validating it or extending it in some way can mean that you embark on a learning journey together.

A woman in her twenties told me recently, when discussing this point, that she distinctly remembers as a child *often* feeling that the adult interacting with her was being patronizing by showing false interest or assuming she wasn't capable. She asserted, "I think children *know*!"

Again, the idea of the adult being a scaffold around the child's learning enables them to progress further than they would do by themselves. Vygotsky calls this the zone of proximal development.

We actually have children at church for a very small amount of time each Sunday and so they deserve to have our complete attention when they are with us. This also gives them the message that they are important to us and their interests have merit because what interests them interests us also.

Involvement levels

As we observe children, how can we tell if what they are doing is purposeful and helpful for them?

This has been the subject of much research and we have drawn ideas from Ferre Laevers' involvement scale[1] for young children and from the EEL project.[2] Using their methods, it is possible to quantify how involved children are in activities and thereby make comparisons and draw conclusions. This is important because there is evidence to suggest that a highly involved child is learning at a deep level and is drawing on complex cognitive processes. As we learn to observe more acutely, we can provide an ever-increasing quality of provision for children at church.

When watching a child during a session, make a mental note of whether you can observe any signals that may indicate that the child is highly involved, such as:

- Concentration
- Energy
- Complexity and creativity
- Facial expression and posture
- Persistence

- Precision
- Reaction time
- Language
- Satisfaction

Laevers talks of five levels of involvement but here we shall look at three broader ones:

1. Low activity

This is where the child's behaviour is repetitive, they are very easily distracted, they are fairly passive, look bored and there is no energy.

2. Mainly continuous activity

Here the child is busy at an activity but it is fairly routine, there is some progress but little energy, and the child is distracted easily.

3. Sustained, intense activity

The child functioning at this level is focusing closely on the activity, much energy is expended and little will distract the child, as their whole concentration is absorbed by the activity. They are using a lot of effort which might be expressed by loud talking, pressing down hard on the paper or by deep thinking. The child is functioning at the height of their capabilities. They are showing attention to detail, taking special care. They might express satisfaction or that it has been important to them, verbally or by using body language. Many of the signals listed above will be present.

These cues from children tell us clearly how involved they are in the activities that we provide for them.

It is important during our children's church that if most of the time, most of the children are exhibiting low involvement levels and their body language tells you they are not engaged – their behaviour is mostly flitting like a butterfly or disruptive – then positive action needs to be taken to change what is offered. We are here to serve the children and provide for their needs, not to make them fit into our programme.

If most of the time most of the children are deeply engaged and engrossed in what they are doing, then broadly speaking, the activities that are provided are at the right level and are interesting to them. That then leaves us free to focus on those few children who need extra support and listening to, so that we can accommodate their different interests.

Supporting children in resolving their conflicts

(It's not about saying sorry!)

Children and adults have conflicts, which are an inevitable part of socializing and being part of a group. Learning how to deal with disagreements and hurt from other people is a really important part of growing up and learning how to stay in relationship in a community.

The challenges we have in a church setting are that it largely meets only once a week, different adults have responsibility for the same group of children and might be adjudicating differently, and it might be the first time a conflict arises when the parent or carer is absent.

So how can we provide consistent care and consistent messages for these very significant events that are bound to occur?

A good attitude to adopt is that this is a positive opportunity for teaching important life skills to young children that will go on equipping them in their adult life. It is a chance for them to learn how to solve problems. It does not mean that children are bad or selfish, just that they are human. They are also learning how to interpret social cues, how to share, how to stand in somebody else's shoes and see another's viewpoint.

One issue that needs to be addressed initially, and I think is rather a red herring, is that of "saying sorry". Interestingly, the word "sorry" appears very little in the Bible and where it does appear, it is linked to repentance,[3] which means to "turn around", which is actually what is desired in the context of following a wrong path, rather than conflicts between people.

It is indeed fascinating to see the many different ways the catch-all word "sorry" is used: as a magic word that immediately turns away anger or a telling off, a word that can get you out of any situation without facing the consequences, an insincere word that can be used to taunt, or a word that genuinely expresses regret and wanting to restore relationship. From the point of view of the person who says sorry, it can be helpful, or the word can be repeated many times over and can effectively be used to berate themselves, but with the danger of never moving on to feel the release of forgiveness. And yet, as adults we often focus on the "sorry" word and miss the attitude change or resolution of an issue, which is really what is needed.

Once again, it is the process that is gone through, the journey to the resolution that is important, rather than just the end of the discord.

Therefore I feel that to focus solely on the end word "sorry" can be misleading rather than addressing the real issue, which is to resolve the source of conflict so that all parties can remain in relationship and sort out the problem.

I have worked in a very large nursery (240 children a day with a large teaching team) where the whole setting adopted the same strategy for supporting children in resolving their conflicts. It was based on respecting all the children involved and helped them to find their voice to express themselves, and it worked well in finding a pathway through to a solution. The whole teaching team used the same methodology, so there was consistency wherever the children were and whoever they were involved with.

On reflection, I wished that I had learned this as a pattern earlier in my own life, and I am still learning to put it into practice.

The method I have used successfully with children is from HighScope,[4] who have developed a six-step process to solve problems and resolve conflicts.

The six steps

1. Approach calmly

Approach at the children's level, not towering over them, and stop any hurtful actions or language. Remove and hold any object that might be the source of conflict in order to neutralize it. Use a calm manner in order to give assurance that all will be resolved fairly.

2. Acknowledge feelings

Children need to express their feelings before they can let go of them and think about possible solutions to the problem. Support them by saying things like "I can see that you are upset…" and addressing each one individually.

3. Gather information

Be careful not to take sides but gather information, allowing each child to explain what happened in their own words. Ask open-ended questions. Other children who were present can also contribute. Take particular care with children who are less verbal and keep checking with them for accuracy of their view.

4. Restate the problem

The adult restates the problem, using simple terms but removing any hurtful or provocative language.

5. Ask for ideas for solutions and choose one together

Be ready to stay with this step for a while and have confidence in asking the children to come up with solutions. These need to be practical and acceptable to all concerned. Be careful not to force them to "all play together again", as this might not be their solution or the best solution either. Check carefully that all children have had an equal voice and all agree with the solution. As this happens, emphasize that they have solved the problem and have done well.

6. Give follow-up support as needed

Help the children as they begin to carry out their solution and give support for any child who is still feeling upset. It might be necessary to go back and repeat some of the steps.

HighScope have made a very useful "fly on the wall" video,[5] which clearly shows some very real conflicts between young children and how this practical method can be seen to work successfully.

From a personal point of view, it took me a while to learn how to put the steps into practice – I even carried a prompt note – but surprisingly, this method fitted all the situations I came across, and was incredibly helpful. I found it to be non-judgmental and it prevented the common mistake of an adult seeing half the event and drawing wrong conclusions. I also found it respectful of all children, and even those with little language were able to benefit as other children alongside got involved. The adult stops being the all-powerful decision-maker but instead supports the children with skill as they learn to find their own solutions. This teaches the children independence skills and helps them to take responsibility rather than waiting passively for an adult to solve things. Children become empowered to be problem-solvers rather than helpless victims.

Steps 2, 3 and 4 gave the children time to calm down, which is essential, as with high emotions their brains are awash with adrenaline that evokes the fight-or-flight response. During this phase, the cortex, the higher brain levels, are not available for thinking and processing the issue at hand, so calming down is necessary.

Step 5 of the process takes time and requires a confidence in the children's ability to think of solutions. And what never ceased to amaze me were the unpredictable resolutions that children came up with that gratified all concerned. Rarely were they anything that I would have dreamt of suggesting and yet they were appropriate and worked.

In church, after a conflict arose, I followed up by explaining what had happened earlier, to the parents of all concerned, so that if the children should need more support after the session ended, then their parents were in the picture.

A criticism of this method is that it takes time.

It initially does! But I see it as a real investment of an important strategy in young lives. However, it does not always take a long time and I have found rich rewards when I have observed children going through the process themselves unsupported. They really listen to the questions that the adults ask and repeat them in context at a later date.

This is just as important as learning about Bible stories.

I believe this is closer to the pattern we learn from Jesus when he reinstates Peter,[6] which is all about restoring a strong relationship on a sound foundation – the foundation-stone, Petros, on which the church would be built.

Adopting this consistent approach among the team addresses all the challenges raised originally concerning children's experience in church and the variety of adults involved. This process can be clearly communicated to all parents – for example, in the "Welcome" leaflet (see below).

Relationships with parents

Communication before the child enters the group

All communication with parents needs to be genuinely respectful, as they are the most important and enduring educators and influencers of their child. They also know their child better than anyone else does. Transparency and honesty are essential values.

Children in the Way?

It can be very helpful to create a "Welcome to Children's Church" leaflet or letter to ensure that all essential points are covered with each family and nothing is forgotten. We might also need to bear in mind that not all families read or are able to read English, and so a culturally relevant alternative means of communication might be necessary.

Points to cover in your "Welcome" leaflet/letter:

- A warm welcome.

- Your aims and values for children in children's church.

- The starting ages for each group.

- Procedure for starting: the parent stays with the child for at least the first session and until they settle.

- Who the leaders or helpers are, and that they have been police checked.

- Hand-over procedures at the beginning and end of each session.

- A normal pattern for the session.

- Possible programme information.

- What clothing to wear (able to get messy).

- Health and safety issues.

- Which words their child uses to ask for the toilet.

- Any allergies the child has.

- Any health issues the child has that the adults need to be aware of.

- Any special educational needs that the child may have.

- What special interests the child has.

- Any insights that the parent wants to share about their child.

- Any worries the parent may have.

- How the rota is arranged and what the parent's part is.

In that leaflet there are some discussion points, and so it is best for a leader to be able to speak to the families and carefully document information that needs to be shared with the rest of the team a few weeks before they are due to start. Also, any special interests the child has could be catered for in their first session.

Some young children arrive at church, brought by slightly older siblings, and so it is most important to communicate with the parents or carers. A home visit to make respectful contact can reap dividends and pave the way for a future relationship.

When a child and parent start together in the group, it is important to make them feel welcomed but not the focus of attention. Starting with a drink and fruit can ease all the children in happily. Encourage parents to join in with whatever their child is interested in, and later they might feel more comfortable being directed to join in with an activity. Make sure that you spend time playing alongside their child, sensitively making connections where possible. At the end of the first session reflect with the parent how you think that went and what approach to employ the next week.

Allow the child to be the guide so that the transition to being left is appropriate and peaceful.

Some families are very keen to leave the child quickly – for example, when there is a new baby and they feel exhausted, but may fail to understand the enormous impact a new baby has on the older sibling. In fact the arrival of a new family member is a major adjustment for the other siblings, and a previously confident and outgoing child may well need much more reassurance and affirmation from their parents and might find children's church one step too far for a short period of time.

Observation has taught me that a happy transition is a gradual one, and following the pace set by the child has long-term benefits. A transition that pushes the child faster than they want to go leads to prolonged anxiety and generally achieves the opposite effect.

Giving positive feedback

At the hand-over time try to be available to talk to parents about what their child has enjoyed through the session. Include friendships as well as activities so that they can follow these up if they wish to. I draw upon my observations of their child's learning and the connections they make, and try to feed those back to the parents or carers, valuing the importance of their thinking. This has often led to fuller discussions about their child's interests at home, all of which are useful for weaving into the future planning of sessions. From a parent's perspective, I know how wonderful it is when somebody appreciates something about my child and also "knows" them in a deeper way.

Be clear, honest and positive about any issues that have arisen. If there has been some problem solving around addressing conflicts, then be careful to explain the process again and how it was handled, without attributing blame. Remember that all conflict resolution is a learning opportunity, and is normal in any group situation. Some parents feel very vulnerable and need reassurance that everything has been fully resolved and that all the children have been respected equally. Others can respond more assertively, and we might need to use conflict resolution skills ourselves! However, remembering that it is never good to label children and that each session needs a fresh start, I have found it helpful to discuss any issues in a matter-of-fact way.

As relationships develop, some parents confide issues that they might be struggling with personally. Confidentiality is highly important, however, and there might be opportunities for pastoral support from other services available from the church.

All relationships are important and need to be valued highly. There needs to be equality of respect for everyone, regardless of age, gender, ethnicity, faith, length of time in the church or role within the church.

Reflection

- Casting my mind back to when I was between the ages of three and seven, can I remember a person who made me feel good about myself or gave me confidence?
  - *What did they do or say that helped convey that message?*
  - *How did they do or say it?*
  - *Can I learn from that to develop my communication skills with children?*
- Reflecting on my own childhood, can I remember a conflict I was involved in that was handled badly by an adult?
  - *What happened?*
  - *How could it have been handled better?*
  - *How could you use that experience to benefit the children you are with?*

- Return to an incident in your childhood when a sharp disagreement was handled well by an adult.
  - *What happened?*
  - *What did the adult do well?*
  - *What was the positive impact for you?*
  - *How could you incorporate constructive points in your own contact with children?*

CHAPTER 11

It's About Time!

Carrie

In order to begin making decisions about the spaces and materials we have available to us as a children's church, it is helpful to lay out some principles or aims and decide what good-quality provision looks like. This may feel like blue-sky thinking, but if we have a clear idea of the very best, then we can select elements of that for the situations we are in, and know that even the little we offer is of good quality.

The resources are there to support learning that the children can actively engage with using their senses and developing skills. Later on, when we add in the rich vehicle of stories and events from the Bible, the children can respond using the resources available to them. Sometimes the responses will be clearly linked to the story and at other times they will not be. This is valid for two reasons. First, children often need time to process new experiences and new thinking before it is reflected in their play. Secondly, they might be engaged in learning something completely different at the time, such as: "How can I play with my friend? How do I negotiate sharing? How can I process the change in circumstances at home?" Although this is not linked to the planned programme, it is valid that this type of reflection can happen during church time.

Too often funding for the children's work is minimal and families' discarded and tired toys are relegated to the boxes that appear in children's church. It's time to call a halt on that method of recycling, even though the intentions are kind. I wonder how the musicians in the churches we are in would feel if they had to create music with a discarded pile of broken and tattered instruments. And it's also time we had a fresh look at the children's spaces provided and the materials they are offered. Some radical changes are needed.

However, on what basis do we make decisions?

Is it about buying new stuff?

Let's start with some sound principles of what types of materials children need in order to learn and express themselves creatively and actively. In order to do that, we need to understand how children learn.

Ingredients of active learning

Active learning is when children are able to engage with activities in an interactive way and using all of their senses. In order for this to happen certain provisions need to be made.

Choice

Motivational research[1] shows that children's intrinsic motivation to learn is greater in activities that they select themselves. By offering a range of good choices which children then select from, their interest is almost guaranteed. This also teaches them the ability to make decisions for themselves and can increase their self-confidence.

Materials

We need to offer a wide range of materials which can be used in a variety of ways. These need to be open-ended rather than prescriptive. For example, we could offer: paper of different colour, sizes and textures, neatly arranged for children to select from, rather than an adult-made cut-out shape which immediately shuts down creative possibilities and dictates much of the end product. Open-ended resources can be used in a myriad ways that stimulate more thinking and wider learning opportunities.

Manipulation

Give children the freedom to create and explore the things that they are interested in.

Let them discover the properties of materials: sticky, rough, smooth, heavy, springy.

Help them learn useful skills: cutting, sticking, joining, folding, tying.

Help them discover concepts and relationships: above, below, same, different, size, fitting together, inside, full and empty – all through exploratory play.

Language

Providing children with opportunities for active learning will result in their language being developed. When they have chosen their own activities and begin to engage with them, they talk to themselves (sometimes out loud), to each other and to interested adults about what they are doing, what they need, how they are doing it and also about totally unrelated ideas.

However, with strongly adult-led activities their talking shuts down as they focus on following instructions and getting it "right". Their anxiety levels tend to rise and they are more easily frustrated and distracted. Therefore complex adult-led activities need to be kept to a minimum. It is fine to introduce new methods – e.g. how to use wax crayons and thin paint to produce wax-resist effects, or how to use the glue effectively – but not how to follow a long list of steps in order to produce a satisfying outcome.

Support

The adult becomes a partner in their play, talking to them in that context, listening closely to them. Instead of solving children's problems that arise, the adult models thinking steps and scaffolds the child to help them solve their own problems. For example: a child is playing with the bricks and farm animals but is frustrated by the roof, which keeps collapsing. The adult might say: "I wonder what else you could use for a roof?… What do you think would fit?… I wonder if your friend could suggest an idea?" (This last question is because the most powerful learning tool is to teach somebody else how to do something, so asking another child for help enables that child to benefit.) The adult observes closely and at times reflects back to the child the steps they have made and at other times adds questions that challenge thinking and extend the play along the same path.

Results of active learning

Children are engaged

When children have been given free choice, they are much more likely to be interested in what they have chosen. They are therefore more likely to remain involved with their task. This has been the findings of research using such indicators as their involvement levels.[2] In addition, they are more often functioning using higher cognitive skills and their play is more complex.

Children gain self-confidence

Children discover that they can make decisions and follow ideas through. They find that they can complete things, and in doing so overcome problems with solutions. They learn that there are no right or wrong ways of doing things necessarily, but rather that there are problems to solve.

Children develop independence

As children learn that they are decision makers and problem solvers, so they become more independent – and independent thinkers as well. They learn not to rely too much on others to tell them how, when or why. This is important as they will need independent and reflective thinking skills as they enter the teenage years. They will need these competencies and strength of character not to follow the crowd but make their own choices. (See the HighScope Perry Preschool project for exciting longitudinal research results that verify the above claims.)[3]

In short, they will become lifelong learners, where once again it is the journey or the process that is important.

Knowledge nowadays is much more accessible than it was for previous generations and can be accessed through the click of a mouse. So the crucial issue is how that knowledge is used, and for that we need children to develop high-level thinking skills.

Looking at Jesus and his teaching methods, we discover that he often told stories which provoked further thinking. They needed mulling over and exploring. They often worked on different levels and rewarded those who ardently pursued the nugget inside. It required an individual journey to be embarked on, a quest or a hunger for more. Helping our children to think and ask questions as well as teaching them from a rich reservoir of stories, can set them up for a life of faith and relationship with God.

Creative spaces inside

Crouch down to the children's height and look at the environment available to your three to seven year olds.

What can you see?

Is it inviting?

Ideally, it should feel warm and welcoming.

Does it draw you in?

There needs to be a cosy area for sitting quietly and looking at books, and an area for messy activities such as sand and water, paint and glue, with a floor surface that is easy to clean. Construction equipment such as wooden blocks do well on a rug or carpet, as it is comfortable to kneel on and reduces the noise. The equipment should be near an imaginative play area such as role play or small-world play, as it can be used to extend the play there. And lastly, there needs to be a table with correctly sized chairs, and access to mark-making resources. There is no need to have one chair for each child, as the only time they will all be sitting together to explore a story is in the cosy book area on cushions.

... And outside!

Outside areas can also be developed creatively. Ideally, there would be a climbing area, space to run and a defined space for wheeled vehicles and for using small equipment such as balls. There also need to be a quiet area and places to hide or chat with a friend. Obviously, access to the natural world will be enhanced if various plants are allowed to thrive and the children are encouraged to garden. The outside has such potential for large-scale construction and imaginative play as well as an area for sand, water and mud.

Quality resources

At the risk of being disheartening, I shall nevertheless describe what the best-quality resources might look like, knowing that the majority of churches will not have anything like this available to them. However, it is essential to be able to visualize excellence clearly, and it is amazing to see how a barren space, over a period of time, can be magically transformed little by little.

Quality, rather than quantity, is crucial to give the message to children that they are valued, and we need to make the resources usable.

Therefore get rid of all the dirty, handed-down rubbish that is kindly given, recycled even, but unpleasant to use. Declutter the space that you have autonomy over. Somehow the plastic rubbish seems to wash up in these places like some polluted beach.

Here is a "blue-sky thinking" list of quality resources for children's church groups:

- A quiet area with a rug and cushions with a low-level bookcase and a small number of books, both secular and Christian. Remove any tattered books, as they will give the message that books can be treated badly and that the readers only deserve the dregs. Remove any cushions that smell or that you would not like to sit on, as children's sense of smell is keener than ours. Make sure cultural diversity is clearly represented in the books as wherever we are living, we are part of a multicultural society.

- A wall-mounted chalkboard at the children's level, with chalks and a board rubber.

- A wall-mounted mirror at children's height gives the reflected message that "You belong here."

- Water play in a tray. Waterproof aprons on pegs nearby for children to use independently. A stack of baskets nearby to hold various resources such as jugs of different sizes, funnels, containers, a water-wheel. This can be simply enhanced by adding dye or bubbles to the water.

- Sand (wet or dry) available in a sand-tray or container that a group of children can gather round. A stack of baskets nearby with sand toys: spades, forks, rakes, buckets, cars, diggers. Less is more here; keep only the items that are satisfying to use.

- Low tables for use with paints/glue/clay/other media. I prefer these to easels, which never stack away easily, are harder for children to use independently and can only be used for painting. Children seem to prefer using paint on a horizontal surface, as it does not run down in great drips. There do not have to be many tables or chairs, as much of children's play will be on the floor and rarely will they all sit down at once, except for the story, which will be on the rug (see above).

- A selection of tubs of different and interesting materials such as bits of fabric, wooden off-cuts, cardboard recycled objects, buttons, bottle-tops, ribbons, laces etc.

- A bowl of warm water, soap and a towel for children to clean up after themselves.

- A drying rack for wet creations at children's level for them to use independently.

- Paper of different shapes, colours and textures, for self-selection.

- Mark-making materials: sharpened pencils, satisfying crayons, pastels, chalks, oil pastels, felt pens (but only if they work; otherwise remove them). The best felt pen storage device is a wooden block with lots of holes the same diameter as the felt pens. It's neat, it's easy to see when one is missing, and no lids get lost.

- Tools: scissors, masking tape (easy to use and tear and paint over), a hole punch, treasury tags.

- Big bricks and smaller bricks / train track, for construction on a thin rug, to reduce noise levels.

- Construction equipment on a rug. It is better to have a lot of one type of equipment, as it is more satisfying to use rather than a small amount of many different types.

- A role-play area with a few quality props related to the story. This is the hardest place to keep tidy and therefore user friendly. Only introduce props that can belong somewhere specific rather than in a heap. Props can include home utensils, dressing-up clothes and hats. Again, less is more, and clothes can be rotated, depending on the current topic. Make sure you have interesting male as well as female clothes to select from. Make sure that cultural diversity is clearly represented here, whatever the origins the families come from.

- Small-world objects: people (reflecting ages and diversity), cars, trains, animals etc.

- A digital camera: for recording children's expressions through creative play. Display the pictures with annotations so that both children and parents can see clearly what is valued and celebrated. Using their own photos in a display (providing the right permissions have been given) gives the clear message to the child: "I can see myself here, I belong here." The camera can also capture the all-important *process* of learning and the child's engagement, sometimes using the camera screen or email rather than having the expense of printing pictures.

- A builder's tray: this is a large octagonal, tough tray that builders use to mix cement. For us it provides just the right size of tray for a group of children to gather round and explore imaginative stories using changeable resources. (See the picture below.)

- Open-fronted, low-level shelves for children to be able to see clearly displayed and labelled resources from which to make their selection.

- Displays of the children's own work when they have decided on the end product. Include photos of each child, as this enables them to see that they belong and are represented in this place. Of course, this is dependent on obtaining permission, and on whether there are other users of the space. Alternatively, store the photo display in a locked cupboard.

- An outside area: to be used in all weathers with many of the resources inside provided outside as well, but able to be used on a grander scale and in louder ways. In addition, there need to be spaces to hide away in and make dens, spaces to sit and chat with a friend, spaces to use large-scale construction using large muscles, and spaces to move fast and use balls and other small equipment.

The equipment here need not be expensive: milk crates, recycled boxes, tyres, shells, pieces of guttering and plastic piping, hoses, watering cans, flower pots, seed trays, trowels and other tools, buckets, a picnic set, dressing-up clothes, rugs, blankets, a clothes-horse, metal saucepans, rolls of paper, paint brushes, a box of books.

Sand, clay and water are very important for the three-to-seven age group, as they are continuous materials and offer the chance of a therapeutic, tactile experience as children process their feelings and experiences. They are also an important vehicle for exploration and experimentation, provoking rich language and the understanding of mathematical concepts, as well as presenting social opportunities for playing alongside others, leading to cooperative play. These materials do not demand a finished product and so are less threatening. There is often much resistance to having these rather tactile resources available indoors, but in my view the benefits far outweigh any untidiness. Children can also be taught how to clear up effectively – another chance to learn an independence skill.

It will mean more work for us – but who are we there for?

Is the building more important than the children?

The painting, drawing and gluing activities give free reign to children's imagination and exploratory drive, and sometimes are the only opportunity they have to explore messier, creative activities.

Children in the Way?

A role-play area, bricks and small-world play allow the children to literally step into somebody else's shoes and gain understanding through imaginative play. They can be used to rehearse important events in the child's life or for playing out stories. Research has suggested that children who had these chances removed when they were seven and under were less able to write well when tackling subjects such as history and English at secondary school level.

> During my teaching at infant school level, a highly articulate child in my class very sadly lost his mum to cancer. Over the next several months he took the opportunities I gave him to play with big bricks, which he used to create coffins, and then he lay down in them. He was working out his grief through play. This was serious business of great importance and a wholly helpful and purposeful process for him to go through.

Therefore we need to adjust our understanding of what "play" means. It is the stuff of life through which children access the world, learn how it works and where they fit in. It is also where they play out their family and other important relationships.

A builder's tray has a wide variety of uses. In the story of the lost sheep, for example, I used rocks, peat, grass, sand with evergreen fronds stuck in to represent trees, and some plastic sheep to hide in the different terrains. For Daniel and the lions' den, I used mostly rocks and sand and evergreen branches and plastic lions. For the Garden of Eden, I added a range of herbs and flowers to select from, a pond (water in a shallow tray), sand and peat, and plastic wild animals for the children to create their own Eden.

Displays of children's work give a strong message to them that "I value highly what you have created." Thinking of modern art, we need to have a broader perspective of what we display, rather than thinking it has to look like something; and make sure, over time, that every child's work is included.

Outside spaces are highly important for young children, as has been discussed earlier. If there is outdoor space at all, it can transform children's church experiences into mostly positive ones. Jesus was outside most of the time and drew on nature around him to illustrate his teaching. He said, "Consider the lilies", when they were sitting where? Amongst the lilies on a hillside! He said, "I will make you fishers of men" by the lake; "A shepherd lost a sheep" to a farming community; and "A sower went to sow his seed" while overlooking some fields.

Builder's Tray

It is not very natural to be predominantly indoors in confined spaces, and this gives rise to far more conflict. Admittedly, the climate was different for Jesus, but in Scandinavian countries parents and carers manage to stay outside with young children for hours at a time, so the rest of us can do it too.

Again, it comes down to the questions;

- How will the children benefit?
- What is best for the children?

There is so much to learn from looking at the world of nature that can't be gained from plastic imitations or second hand: the wonder of metamorphosis, the importance of weeding and pruning, the promise of a rainbow.

Where do I go from here?

Some churches are lucky enough to have a designated room for young children's sole use, and any resources can be left there for the next week. In which case, audit the resources you have and get rid of tatty materials and bits and pieces that will never get used.

The organization needs to be like a beautiful art shop: all neatly laid out with a wide choice – for example, different types of paper tempting you to come and touch, come and buy! Less is more, rather than "Stack it high and sell it cheap". There is a wonderful art shop near my home where marvellous materials invite you to pick them up and imagine how they could be used, like some sumptuous banquet with mouth-watering dishes. When I am there time enters another dimension, and invariably I come out with new ideas. Children too need to feel as if they are in Aladdin's cave, where they can choose from treasures to explore. However, resources do not have to be expensive, as they should be the basic building blocks which children then use to create their own worlds.

Perhaps your church will only have tiny amounts of space and no storage facilities at all, and so all the materials have to be brought in each week. I have been in your situation too.

If there were only four pieces of equipment that I could have, I would choose: a camera, for the reasons above; some blankets or rugs; a trolley with six tubs containing different choices for the children, which is transportable and changeable each week; and the ever-variable builder's tray. Each week the contents of the tubs would change, clearly labelled, and I would try to incorporate resources that matched the interests of the particular children I had.

In a large hall, for example, I have found that rugs or blankets are useful tools. The children choose a tub which is labelled, for example, "Treasure", with a picture label too. They take that tub to a rug which is comfortable to sit on and helps them settle. The treasure (linked to "The Ten Talents" or "The Precious Pearl") is costume jewellery/bric-a-brac/mirrors covered with water for the children to explore. The rugs help them get down on the floor and focus on what they have selected. Blankets can also be used, draped over chairs or clothes-horses, to create tents or dens.

Questioning skills: "A time to be silent and a time to speak" (Ecclesiastes 3:7)

A friend recounted the following anecdote. She was in church, and an adult was doing "the children's slot" and was describing something and asking the children to guess what it was: "It's got a long bushy tail, climbs trees and likes nuts... What is it?"

A confident child responded, "I know the answer is Jesus, but it sounds just like a squirrel to me!"

This child knew what the usual answer was!

Children very quickly pick up the expected response, but is there something we can do to stimulate deeper thinking in even our youngest children?

Whatever other resources you do or don't have, by far the most powerful and important resources are the adults working with the children.

This is so important, it is worth saying again:

By far the most powerful and important resources you have are the adults working with the children.

Their impact can transform experiences for children and enrich their lives. As has already been discussed, tuning in closely to children throughout the session is essential and communicates the hidden message that they and their interests are worthwhile and valued highly. As the quote from Ecclesiastes above says, there is a time to speak and a time to be silent, and we need wisdom to know when to do what. It is imperative to truly listen to what children are saying and give value to their responses, rather than bombarding them with myriad questions. However, a timely question can evoke productive thinking.

If we are committed to improving on our previous best practice, how can we improve the quality of communication between adults and children in the time we have them on a Sunday?

An important skill that can easily be developed is the type of questions that are asked. All of us have a range of questions that we naturally draw on, but there are many more that we can learn to use that can stimulate children to think more deeply or more widely and make important connections between one area of learning and another. One helpful way of categorizing questions has been done by the Websters[4] in a book for which I was a consultant.

Types of questions

There is a time and place for all of these questions:

Closed questions

These require a "yes" or "no" response. A minimal response which hardly challenges the children's thinking but increases their chance of getting it wrong. E.g.: "Is this a Bible?"

When you need to know quickly whether there is anybody left in the burning building, then a closed question is best! Or when I want the whole group to chorus in a knowing way: "Can you remember what to put on before using the paints?" Chorus: "An apron!" When I have a purpose in mind, such as helping an anxious child to come and join the group, I might ask: "Would you like to sit next to Archie or me?", in order to give them a narrow choice and help them over the hurdle of sitting down, rather than: "Do you want to join the group?"

Display questions

These ask for information which the adult already has. They are often interpreted by children as requests to talk – e.g. "What colour are your shoes?" – or to see if they understand something – e.g. "How many fingers am I holding up?" The children know they are being tested.

Display questions are understood as a social convention that children learn to deal with: "Whose birthday is it today, then?" I always think of Joyce Grenfell the actress and her marvellous voice with these sorts of questions, which she used in her imaginary classroom, and that generally steers me away. They might be useful for checking between you and the child that you both are agreed on a course of action: "Do you remember where we are going next?"

Factual questions

These are checking out what the children have recalled: e.g. "What did Zacchaeus do first? Then what happened next?" They reflect many adults' concerns to exert a high degree of control over what children learn and do.

Factual questions might help in certain sorts of tests or learning by rote, but they generally tend to increase anxiety and eat away at confidence. Some church traditions highly value learning verses or references, and it might be applicable for older groups. However, in terms of young children's spiritual development and their growing awareness of a loving heavenly Father who they already belong to, it is more to do with relationship than head knowledge.

Open questions

These give full scope for recalling an event and constructing a reply. They are inhibiting to many children with immature language. E.g.: "What did you do this weekend?"

I have often heard it said that we need to ask "open-ended" questions. These can sometimes be effective, but it depends on the child.

> On collecting my son Josh from school, then aged four, if I asked, "What did you do at school today?", I would be asking an open-ended question – but the answer I invariably got was, "Nothing!" I think he felt he'd been there, done that and worked hard, and it was just too exhausting to rehash the whole day for me.
>
> On the other hand, if I was collecting my daughter Rebecca from school at the same age, asking the same question would be like turning on a tap, for out would pour a torrent of all the events and nuances of what had happened – who said what to whom, and the sort of earrings the teacher had on, the mood she was in and how Rebecca felt with her friends at play time.
>
> Actually, now I come to think of it, they are much the same today and they are both in their twenties!

Divergent questions

These have more than one right answer, e.g. "I wonder what do you think is in this parcel?… What do you think would happen if…? What else could we try…? I wonder how you would feel if…?" These questions encourage children to make predictions, to express personal feelings, and to give more of their own ideas.

Cognitively challenging questions

These help children to think about their learning activities. They are genuine requests for accounts, reasons or explanations. E.g. "Which was the harder of those two towers to make?… How did you know when it was cooked?… What have you discovered about pouring water into the sand?… Does this story remind you of another story?"

The exciting aspect of these last two, more challenging (and better) types of questions is that children's responses are usually interesting and unpredictable. I love finding out how children's minds work and the connections they make. They also relax as they understand they are not being tested and so can't get something wrong or be made to feel embarrassed, but gradually realize that their ideas are being valued.

I often start a session by putting a small object connected to the story into a bag, and asking the children to feel inside and guess what it might be. Alternatively, I might put a larger object in the middle of the group and cover it up.

> For example, I borrowed a budgie in a cage (the "God made birds" session) and covered it over with a blanket and asked the children, "I wonder what you think might be under the blanket?" And I always replied positively and allowed every child a guess who wanted to. Some of the guesses were logical – e.g. "a teddy" or "a rabbit" – to which I replied, "Good idea!" or "Good thinking!" or "It might be!" And others were imaginary – e.g. "An elephant!" – to which I replied, "That's a wonderful idea!" I asked them if they could hear anything, and if they had heard a sound like that before, and if they could smell anything, encouraging them to use their senses, as young children's sense of smell is often keener than ours.

In general, a good way to start questions is; "I wonder…" as it invites a wide range of ideas and stimulates thinking.

A general rule of thumb is: *If you know the answer to the question, then don't ask it!*

Old habits die hard and our speech patterns are no exception to that.

Fold your arms in front of your chest. Now try to fold them the other way!

How does that feel?

Most people report that it feels awkward and uncomfortable. However, if you practised folding your arms the "wrong" way for two weeks, it would feel just as normal as the other way.

And so it is with questions.

Therefore, in order to adopt new ways of interacting with children, it will take practice and it might feel a little odd at first. However, in terms of enriching the children's experience and making it a more interesting session for the adults as well, it can be invaluable.

In order to facilitate the team's developing expertise, questions should be added to the planning. This is for two reasons: firstly, it is easier to think of new ideas during some quiet thinking time; and secondly, it really is *that* important.

If everybody in the team knew the couple of important questions to ask each session, then the experience would be more satisfying from the child's perspective and the ethos would be more cohesive as well.

Although many churches will start off with rather spartan material resources, we should remember once again that the most important resources are the adults who interact with the children. Having said that, it is possible, little by little, step by step, to achieve enormous changes over a period of time. If change is to happen and money is to be invested in the children's work, how important it is, then, to make sure that it is invested wisely on the best-quality materials for our most precious members.

Reflection

- Draw a plan of your children's church area, including doors, flooring, taps and any permanent structures.
  - *Note the pathways through the space.*
- On another sheet list the inventory of equipment / materials.
  - *Take a fresh look at the available area and only put back equipment and materials that are of good quality and relevant, bearing in mind the principles already discussed.*
  - *Think about where you will put the equipment for easy access by the children.*
  - *Decide what to do with the excess materials.*
  - *Draw up a list, with the team, of prioritized desirable additions (see "Strategies for leading a team" in Chapter 5).*
  - *Creatively think of ways to borrow significant resources for specific sessions.*
- How are your resources stored and labelled?
  - *Can the children access them independently?*
  - *Can the children "read" the picture or word label easily?*
  - *What is on display?*
  - *What is being valued?*
  - *Who is the audience?*
  - *What is at children's height?*
  - *Have you ever seen children interacting with the display?*

- Is there wall space at adults' height for displaying some useful generic questions to help prompt all those working with the group?

    - *Who could you enlist to help you in creating helpful adult prompts?*

CHAPTER 12

Once upon a Time...

Designing a session

Carrie

Jesus was a remarkable teacher and the crowds recognized that he spoke with authority and was somehow very different from the Pharisees,[1] which they found amazing. One of the main vehicles he employed was the medium of story, using everyday examples to communicate spiritual truths. The stories hooked his listeners and had different layers of meaning, so they could be understood on a peripheral level, but also had depths that could be plumbed.

Some of them contained humour that is lost in translation. For instance, the shepherds were the butt of jokes along the lines of "Have you heard the latest 'shepherd' joke?" Some of Jesus' humour was more universal: consider the incongruity of the camel fitting through the eye of a needle.[2]

Also, the stories were memorable and so provided food for thought over the next period of time, should people continue to mull over the meaning.

I can just imagine a farmer, months later, sowing his next crop, suddenly stopping halfway across his field and saying, "Ah, so *that's* what he meant!"[3]

Or a mother reflecting on her love for her children and beginning to dare to think new thoughts about the God of heaven she had always believed in. Could he possibly have a similar love for her – only more so?[4]

Jesus was an extremely good teacher and there is much we can learn from his techniques. Like him, we need to *start with the experience and the world of the listeners* – in our case, the children – with whom we are involved, and then build from there. If we are talking about the story of the wise man building his house on the rock, for example, we need to make sure they have experience of sand, rock, building structures and the effect of rain! These are actually quite adult concepts and completely appropriate for Jesus to talk to people who built their own houses, but our children have generally not watched a house being built or contributed to the process.

Does this mean we should not tell this story?

I think it makes it essential, therefore, to give children the experience of playing with rocks, sand and watering cans and building house structures in order to understand the point of the story. Another strategy with other stories is to take something that is very well understood by our children and adapt the Bible story to fit. For example, the story of the lost coin could be the loss of the special toy or blanket that they have; this refers them back to the feelings of losing something and then the joy of finding it.

Most of the currently available programmes for working with church children are actually stripped-down adults' materials. So what we are suggesting is radical in that we always start with the child, and build from there. The basic point of this book is to give you the research and reasoning that leads us to this place.

So starting with my children at this time and their developmental stage, how can I present them with meaningful connections to powerful stories?

The children that I am involved with might have very diverse experiences compared to the ones you are working with. Therefore it is essential that ideas that are given here are reinterpreted to make them relevant and meaningful to your children, acknowledging different cultures and contexts.

A two-year plan

I designed this plan to roll out over two years, and tried to cover the stories that I loved and felt I could make appropriate for our children. Please use this plan as a starting point only, for you to change and adapt, and include those stories that are special to you. Each year there are different numbers of Sundays in each month, so I have included some months with five Sundays in, but not others, so please adjust the plans accordingly. I focused on different aspects of Christmas each year, and of course Easter is such a moveable feast that alterations will be needed. Each child might be there for three to four years and so will experience repeats – but does this matter?

Not at all!

Each adult is likely to express the story in a unique way and so sessions will not be identical. Children, two years on, will also be different people and will see things from a new perspective but will enjoy any familiarity; and in any case, repetition can aid the reinforcement of their learning.

First Year Plan

Month	1st Sunday	2nd Sunday	3rd Sunday	4th Sunday	5th Sunday
September	Adam and Eve – Garden of Eden	Adam and Eve disobedient – leave garden with clothes	House on the rock	Jesus asleep in boat. Calms the storm	
October	Wedding: water into wine	Loaves and fishes (given by little boy)	Jesus heals blind man (mud)	Jesus heals Jairus' daughter	
November	Lost son	Lost coin	Lost sheep	Angel speaks to Mary. Joseph and Mary on donkey	
December	Jesus is born in a stable	Angels and shepherds. Shepherds visit Jesus	Wise men bring gifts to Jesus	Christmas Break. Family service (all come dressed in own choice of nativity clothes)	Christmas Break
January	Creation. God made: light and dark	God made: land, plants, trees, seeds, fruit	God made: water, sea, fish	God made: birds	God made: land animals
February	God made: me Psalm 139	God rested. Sunday is special	Precious pearl	Look at the lilies and birds – do not worry	
March	Mary anointing Jesus feet (washing feet, soap and bubbles)	Palm Sunday Hosanna!	Jesus – the Last supper	Jesus dies on the cross and is alive again	
April	Easter Break	Easter Break	Noah builds the ark	Animals go in two by two	
May	Noah's ark lands. Rainbow. Be fruitful!	Abram called out and living in tent	Abraham friend of God	Abraham and Sara old but have baby Isaac	Isaac marries Rebekah
June	Jesus and the woman at the well	Friends lower man through roof. Jesus forgives and heals	Zacchaeus	Jesus heals centurion's servant	
July	Jonah	Boy David. Shepherd. Plays harp. Chosen	David and Goliath	David and Jonathan best friends	Good King David. Psalms. Praising God; instruments, singing, dancing

August – summer break.

On Mother's day and similar occasions be very aware of children's personal circumstances and only do what is totally inclusive.

N.B. Use real food, animals, tents, boats and natural materials where possible. Use all of the children's senses. Enjoy!

Special note: If you have just opened this book and turned to these plans, please be aware that they do not stand alone and need to be understood in the context of the ethos and principles explained in the text. Please be encouraged to read further for their full meaning.

Second Year Plan

September,1st Sunday Ruth and Naomi	**September, 2nd Sunday** Ruth and Boaz	**September, 3rd Sunday** Big catch of fish	**September, 4th Sunday** All invited to the feast	**October, 1st Sunday** Good Samaritan	**October, 2nd Sunday** Healing lame man. Walking and dancing and praising God
October, 3rd Sunday Ten lepers healed, only one says thank you	**October, 4th Sunday** Joseph's coat and dreams	**October, 5th Sunday** Joseph and his brothers quarrel. Sold into slavery	**November, 1st Sunday** Joseph in strange land. Potiphar lied. Prison	**November, 2nd Sunday** Joseph rules Egypt. Reunited with brothers	**November, 3rd Sunday** Angel speaks to Mary. Mary visits cousin Elizabeth
November, 4th Sunday Mary and Joseph on the donkey. No room at the inn. Jesus born	**December, 1st Sunday** Angels tell shepherds, baby in a manger. Shepherds visit Jesus	**December, 2nd Sunday** Wise men follow star and bring gifts to Jesus	**December, 3rd Sunday** Christmas Break Family service (all come dressed in own choice of nativity clothes)	**December, 4th Sunday** Christmas Break	**January, 1st Sunday** Jesus as a child left in the Temple
January, 2nd Sunday Jesus baptized by John	**January, 3rd Sunday** Jesus calls his special friends (disciples)	**January, 4th Sunday** The sower and the seed	**January, 5th Sunday** The camel and the little gate	**February, 1st Sunday** Hannah prays for baby Samuel	**February, 2nd Sunday** Hannah loves Samuel but does not live with him
February, 3rd Sunday God speaks to boy Samuel	**February, 4th Sunday** Naaman's slave girl	**March, 1st Sunday** Jesus teaches us to pray; Abba, Daddy	**March, 2nd Sunday** Jesus walks on the water	**March, 3rd Sunday** Palm Sunday Jesus on donkey, palm branches	**March, 4th Sunday** Jesus washes disciples feet (foot painting and washing)
April, 1st Sunday Jesus – the Last supper	**April, 2nd Sunday** Jesus dies on the cross and is alive again	**April, 3rd Sunday** Easter Break	**April, 4th Sunday** Easter Break	**May, 1st Sunday** Baby Moses in the bulrushes	**May, 2nd Sunday** Moses and the burning bush
May, 3rd Sunday Moses and the plagues. Pharaoh changes his mind	**May, 4th Sunday** Moses leads people out. Crosses red sea	**May, 5th Sunday** Moses and the ten commandments	**June, 1st Sunday** Brave Queen Esther	**June, 2nd Sunday** Daniel and the lions' den	**June, 3rd Sunday** Mary and Martha
June, 4th Sunday Lazarus raised from the dead, Mary and Martha	**July, 1st Sunday** Twins. Jacob tricks Esau and runs away	**July, 2nd Sunday** Jacob's dream. Angels and ladder	**July, 3rd Sunday** Jacob wrestles with God and is reunited with Esau	**July, 4th Sunday** Giants! Joshua and Caleb not scared.	**July, 5th Sunday** Joshua and trumpets. Did what God said. Walls of Jericho fall down

August – summer break.

On Mother's/Father's/Carers' day etc. be very aware of children's personal circumstances and only do what is totally inclusive.

N.B. Use real food, animals, tents, boats and natural materials where possible. Use all the children's senses. Enjoy!

Special note: If you have just opened this book and turned to these plans, please be aware that they do not stand alone and need to be understood in the context of the

A detailed plan

My focus for the children is to provide them with a session that is active and interactive and stimulates many of their senses.

Starting with the story, I try to mull over its distilled essence that would be helpful for my group of children. Sometimes I add another main point for those children who could enjoy the extension.

Then I focus on my particular group of children. Visualizing them, I ask myself:

- How can I help my children to experience this?
- Which senses will they be using?
- How can I make this relevant?

For example, the programme was going through the creation story and this week was "God made light". I took down one of my curtains from home that had black-out fabric for the lining, and brought a torch. During the group time at the start of the session I asked whether anybody wanted to go under the curtain with their friend. It would be all dark – and then I would switch the torch on. The first two volunteered and I can remember their responses clearly: "I can't see my hand!" Then I switched the torch on under the curtain and out came the words "I can see my friend!" It was expressed with such a tone of wonder.

Most of the group took their turn in twos.

Relating their experience to the passage in Genesis about God creating the light suddenly became more relevant to them.

For the next step in the planning I try to think of a starting point that will intrigue and captivate their interest. These are sometimes called "provocations for learning" or "fascination traps". Often it will be something hidden in a bag for them to feel and guess, or a large unexpected item such as a tent (a pop-up version) that we gather in to set the context for the story of Moses or Abraham.

Next I draw up some key questions that are going to stimulate their imaginations and their thinking. These questions are often quite difficult to think of, but are very worthwhile.

I note down any specific resources that might be helpful to augment the story in order to allow time to call upon members of the church family to help me find those resources. In addition to the wide range of creative choices that I always offer the children, I include additional ones that are specific to the story.

Then I suggest a song that might be part of the theme. I haven't included any here as song repertoires are very church-specific and change rapidly. Another strategy is to take a familiar nursery rhyme and change the words: e.g. at Christmas time, "Twinkle, twinkle little star, now I know just what you are. Up above the world so high, showing us where Jesus lies", etc.

Lastly, I suggest any books or images that will be needed to enhance the story. Books are an important resource as they can help focus the children's attention, but they need to be read and held in such a way that everyone can see so that it is a satisfying experience for all to share.

This may need practice in front of a mirror.

There are some who might suggest that books dampen children's imagination or connection with God, but I have not come across any evidence to support this. Conversely, I have found books and images to be a rich stimulus from which children can launch into their own creative and spiritual journeys.

Images too can be a powerful vehicle. For example, I was mulling over the story of Daniel and the lions' den and thinking about the two key points I thought would benefit my group of three and four year olds; the first was that lions were fierce and the second was that God's angels were stronger. Connecting with my particular children, I decided that all of them would have been to Bristol Zoo and seen the sleepy old lions there, and so they knew what they looked like and how large they were. So I found some photographic images of lions roaring with their mouths wide open, displaying their enormous teeth.

Next Sunday, as I told the story to the children, I held up the pictures so they could appreciate how fierce the lions were. The children sat enthralled, tightly gripping their cushions! Then I emphasized how strong God's angel was to shut their mouths, so Daniel was saved. They were thrilled. I had pondered over whether to finish the story as the Bible has it, with the bad guys being thrown into the den and eaten. Would the children be upset? At the time I went with the flow and the baddies were duly punished. This met with cheers! I think the children had a strong sense of good and bad, and liked it when poetic justice was meted out. Afterwards, as always, the children had a wide range of creative options to choose from, and the most popular choices that session were the builder's tray with a den landscape and some plastic small-world lions (parents had been asked to lend some for the session) which they used to retell the story with gusto. And also the chalkboard, attached to the wall at their height, which became covered in a variety of beautifully jagged teeth. Parents took photos of the chalk drawings on their mobile phones when they came at the end of the session.

And just in case you were wondering, I had no complaints about any bad dreams!

On the detailed plan, the extra columns are for administration purposes and the last empty column is blank for the leader with their team to add in their own ideas and passions. Please look out for any terms that I have used that are not relevant to your culture and see this as a starting point that will need adapting.

Ideally, I would like to plan with the whole team before each term starts, but in practice I have not been able to achieve this, as other leaders have been time-poor, so I have served them by providing this support. However, gradually, they have understood the idea of planning in depth under those headings and have then been able to run with it independently and I have only needed to give light back-up support. Therefore I have only given one term's example of detailed planning.

This planning provides a cohesive pattern for the children and gives the whole team a usable framework.

Detailed plans for children's church
3 to 7-year-olds

Date	Leader	Helpers	Story/key point/starting point/questions/creative choices/ specific resources/song/book/image	Team's ideas
September, 1st Sunday			**Story:** Adam and Eve in the Garden of Eden. **Key point:** God gave Adam and Eve good things: a lovely garden, animals, fruit trees; they were happy together **Starting point:** Feely bag* with selection of different fruit. Pass round and respond positively to every suggestion: Yes, it could be..., What a good idea! **Questions:** I wonder, what can you feel in this bag? What do you like doing in a garden? I wonder, what is your favourite animal? If you could choose one animal to have in a beautiful garden with you what would it be? Do you like being in a garden or park in the summer or winter best? **Creative choices:** Builder's tray* set up with peat, sand, rocks. Containers with small flowers, herbs and greenery from which to create a garden. Small world animals/people. **Specific resources:** Variety of fruit, chopping board and suitable knives to chop up with an adult and eat together. Builder's tray (see above). Old white sheet of fabric for fruit prints. Shallow paint trays for paint and dipping fruit into for printing. **Song:** **Book/Image:**	

Special note: If you have just opened this book and turned to these plans, please be aware that they do not stand alone and need to be understood in the context of the ethos and principles explained in the text. Please be encouraged to read further for their full meaning.

Date	Leader	Helpers	Story/key point/starting point/questions/creative choices/ specific resources/song/book/image	Team's ideas
September, 2nd Sunday			**Story:** Adam and Eve – disobedient. You can eat anything you want except the fruit from one tree (NB not an apple tree!). Consequences: they leave the garden. God gives them clothes.	
			Key point: Adam and Eve chose to disobey. We can choose to disobey or be good.	
			Starting point: Feely bag with selection of different fruit (different types from last week) for children to put their hand in and guess. Welcome all guesses warmly.	
			Questions: I wonder, can you guess what might be in the bag? Does it remind you of anything? Have you touched something like this before?	
			Story: I wonder, why might Adam and Eve have wanted to eat the fruit from the tree?...I wonder, why did the snake say those things to Eve?...I wonder, how did God feel?...How do you think Adam and Eve felt after they had eaten the fruit?...Why do you think they hid from God?...Have you ever tried to hide after you did something bad?...Sometimes all of us including grown-ups do bad things; what's the best thing to do then?	
			Creative choices: Playdough for exploration. Snake shapes. Dressing up clothes. Builder's tray set up with peat, sand, rocks and containers with small flowers, herbs and greenery from which to create a garden.	
			Specific resources: Variety of fruit, chopping board and suitable knives to chop up with adult and eat together. Dark sugar paper for fruit printing with light coloured paints. Shallow paint trays for paint and dipping fruit into for printing. Builder's tray.	
			Song:	
			Book/Image:	

Special note: If you have just opened this book and turned to these plans, please be aware that they do not stand alone and need to be understood in the context of the ethos and principles explained in the text. Please be encouraged to read further for their full meaning.

185

Date	Leader	Helpers	Story/key point/starting point/questions/creative choices/ specific resources/song/book/image	Team's ideas
September, 3rd Sunday			**Story:** Houses built on sand/rock. **Key point:** Be wise, do what Jesus says. **Starting point:** Put sand in opaque container with cut off sock on the end so they can't see the sand. Pass it around the circle "Put your hand in and feel. I wonder, what does it feel like to you? I wonder what you can feel in here..." (Always respond positively...what a good guess...yes it does feel like sugar). Then pass round without the sock so they can see it. Eventually give the right answer. **Questions:** I wonder, have you ever seen a house being built?...What kind of things do builders use to build a house?...First of all builders dig down deep in the ground to build foundations for the house. I wonder, why do they that?...Why do you think the foolish man's house fell down? **Creative choices:** Sand play outside/inside: use wooden blocks to build houses on sand/ stone. Then pour water on and see if they fall over. General sand and rock play. Wax resist watery pictures. Building bricks on carpet. **Specific resources:** Sand, blocks, water, watering can. White paper, wax crayons, thin paint or Brusho dye* for wax resist. **Song:** **Book/Image:**	

Special note: If you have just opened this book and turned to these plans, please be aware that they do not stand alone and need to be understood in the context of the ethos and principles explained in the text. Please be encouraged to read further for their full meaning.

Date	Leader	Helpers	Story/key point/starting point/questions/creative choices/ specific resources/song/book/image	Team's ideas
September, 4th Sunday			**Story:** Jesus asleep in boat. Jesus calms the storm. Find inflatable dinghy and tell story sitting in dinghy and make it feel stormy /calm with movement and sound effects. Repeat telling from memory as often as they want! All join in; "Peace! Be still!" **Key point:** Jesus is powerful. Jesus brings peace. **Starting point:** Climb into dinghy. Have you ever been in a boat ? Listen to all who want to talk and share experiences. If you could sail anywhere in a boat where would you like to sail to? **Questions:** I wonder, how could Jesus fall asleep when there was a storm?...Have you ever been in a storm?...Have you ever been frightened in a storm?...What do you do to make you feel better?...Is there anything else you could do? **Creative choices:** Inflatable dinghy – leave available for free use. Water play with objects that float and sink, small boats...try to predict what will happen. Wax resist watery pictures. **Specific resources:** Inflatable dinghy. White paper, wax crayons, thin paint or Brusho dye for wax resist. **Song:** **Book/Image:**	
October, 1st Sunday			**Story:** Jesus at the wedding at Cana. Water into wine. **Key point:** Jesus likes us to be happy. Jesus does amazing things. **Starting point:** Feely bag with some dressing up clothes for wedding e.g. tiara and veil **Questions:** Have you ever been to a wedding?...What did you enjoy?...What happened at the wedding?...What did you not like?...I wonder, why did Mary say to the servants: listen to Jesus?...Why do you think Jesus turned the water into wine?	

Special note: If you have just opened this book and turned to these plans, please be aware that they do not stand alone and need to be understood in the context of the ethos and principles explained in the text. Please be encouraged to read further for their full meaning.

Date	Leader	Helpers	Story/key point/starting point/questions/creative choices/ specific resources/song/book/image	Team's ideas
			Creative choices: Dressing up clothes linked to wedding (remember the boys' outfits too). Put red colouring into the water play and lots of containers for pouring, glitter for adding to gluing activity. Making sandwiches for wedding breakfast and eating them.	
			Specific resources: Wedding paraphernalia (n.b. boys' outfits too), food and implements for making sandwiches (remember allergies), glitter.	
			Song:	
			Book/Image:	
October, 2nd Sunday			**Story:** The feeding of the 5000 (John 6).	
			Key point: Little boy gave Jesus his food. Jesus listens to children. Jesus made it enough for everyone.	
			Starting point: Put fresh bread into opaque paper bag, pass round group, ask them to smell and guess what is inside.	
			Questions: I wonder, what can you smell in here?...Does the smell remind you of something?...Why do you think the little boy gave his food to Jesus?...How do you think the boy felt when everyone had lots to eat?	
			Creative choices: Making sandwiches (NB allergies), children to spread their own and cut them independently. Go outside and have a picnic.	
			Specific resources: Bread, spreads, knives, boards, picnic accessories.	
			Song:	
			Book/Image:	

Special note: If you have just opened this book and turned to these plans, please be aware that they do not stand alone and need to be understood in the context of the ethos and principles explained in the text. Please be encouraged to read further for their full meaning.

Date	Leader	Helpers	Story/key point/starting point/questions/creative choices/ specific resources/song/book/image	Team's ideas
October, 3rd Sunday			**Story:** Jesus made the blind man see. Mud in his eyes. **Key point:** What is it like to be blind? Jesus made him better. **Starting point:** Use blindfold and then feel the face of another child and guess who it is. Only for those who want to have a go. Model it yourself first. OR pass round opaque bag for children to put hand in and feel range of household objects, make a guess then pull it out to see. **Questions:** What do you think it feels like to be blind?...If you were blind what things would you find difficult?...Why do you think Jesus used mud to help the man get better?... What do you think the man loved best about getting better and seeing again? **Creative choices:** Thicken brown paint with flour (to be like mud), put on tray. Children can make patterns using fingers (very tactile and absorbing). If you want carry out mono prints; you can take an image of pattern by gently lying paper on top to touch paint then lifting off. **Specific resources:** Flour, brown paint, blindfold (scarf or aeroplane eye shades). **Song:** **Book/Image:**	
October, 4th Sunday			**Story:** Jesus heals Jairus' daughter. **Key point:** Jesus healed the girl then took care of her with a few friends and her mum and dad, gave her food so she could get strong again. **Starting point:** Teddy in the middle of circle with blanket and glass of water. **Questions:** When you are poorly who looks after you?...What things do they do that looked after you?...Is there anything you specially like to eat when you are poorly?	

Special note: If you have just opened this book and turned to these plans, please be aware that they do not stand alone and need to be understood in the context of the ethos and principles explained in the text. Please be encouraged to read further for their full meaning.

189

Date	Leader	Helpers	Story/key point/starting point/questions/creative choices/ specific resources/song/book/image	Team's ideas
			Creative choices: Role play being ill and/or hospitals. Could also provide food for getting better. **Specific resources:** As much doctor and hospital paraphernalia as you can source. Variety of teddies and dolls, remembering balance of gender and ethnicity. Doctors' and nurses' outfits remembering not to gender stereotype.	
November, 1st Sunday			**Story:** Lost son. **Key point:** God forgives us immediately, as soon as we are sorry. **Starting point:** Builder's tray: tell story and move characters around. **Questions:** When the son left home with all the money, how do you think the father felt?…How do you feel when you have done something naughty?…I wonder, what helps you to feel better again?…Why do you think the son wanted to come home again?…How do you think the father felt when he saw his son? **Creative choices:** Drama: all acting every part (including pigs). All take turns running into the arms of adult. I am sorry (child runs), adult: I forgive you (swings round). Could do food and create the welcome home feast. **Specific resources:** Builder's tray, materials for story landscape, small world pigs. For drama need strong adult to swing children round to feel forgiveness and excitement. Do this outside if possible. **Song:** **Book/Image:**	

Special note: If you have just opened this book and turned to these plans, please be aware that they do not stand alone and need to be understood in the context of the ethos and principles explained in the text. Please be encouraged to read further for their full meaning.

Date	Leader	Helpers	Story/key point/starting point/questions/creative choices/ specific resources/song/book/image	Team's ideas
November, 2nd Sunday			**Story:** Lost coin.	
			Key point: God searches until he finds you.	
			Starting point: Bring my own special teddy and pass round. I lost my teddy but I never stopped looking (elaborate).	
			Questions: Have you ever lost something you loved?...Where did you look for it?...How did you feel ?...Did you ever find it ?...How do you think the woman felt when she found her coin?	
			Creative choices: Add shells/interesting objects to sand tray, bury them in the sand so they can be discovered. Use builder's tray to create another type of landscape, again hide "treasure" to be discovered. Use warm water in water tray, add "jewels" and mirrors for explorative play.	
			Specific resources: Builder's tray, treasure, sand tray with shells/other relevant objects. Jewels such as bracelets and necklaces and mirrors, containers to put them in, add to the water play, the water adds a sparkling fascination.	
			Song:	
			Book/Image:	
November, 3rd Sunday			**Story:** Lost sheep.	
			Key point: God searches until he finds you because he loves you.	
			Starting point: Builder's tray with varied landscape. Hide sheep in terrain. Use small world person as shepherd. Tell story: "sheep, sheep!" Where shall I look ? Follow their directions until it is found. They can retell it and play with it for the rest of the session.	
			Questions: Where shall I look ?... Have you ever been lost?... What happened?... How did you feel?... How were you found again?	

Special note: If you have just opened this book and turned to these plans, please be aware that they do not stand alone and need to be understood in the context of the ethos and principles explained in the text. Please be encouraged to read further for their full meaning.

191

Date	Leader	Helpers	Story/key point/starting point/questions/creative choices/ specific resources/song/book/image	Team's ideas
			Creative choices: Builder's tray for retelling story. Farm animal small world play.	
			Specific resources: Photos of different types of sheep. Farm animals. Rocks, peat, sand, evergreen branches, lid with water to form a pond, grass; use to create clearly defined landscape in which to hide the sheep.	
			Song:	
			Book/Image:	
November, 4th Sunday			**Story:** Angel speaks to Mary. Joseph and Mary on donkey.	
			Key point: God told Mary his son would be born.	
			Starting point: Photos of their mothers/others while pregnant to pass round.	
			Questions: Has anybody got a younger brother or sister? How did you know they were going to be born? What did you do to get ready for the baby? What do you think Joseph and Mary did to get ready for Jesus? Could they take stuff with them? How do you think it felt to ride on a donkey with a very big tummy?	
			Creative choices: Get strong adult/teenager to come and give donkey rides around the room. Stuff cushion up jumper.	
			Specific resources: Strong adult for donkey rides. Baby dolls, male and female, for role play e.g. bathing, feeding, putting to bed (remember to encourage boys as well as girls to play with baby dolls as they need to learn to be good, nurturing dads).	
			Song:	
			Book/Image:	

Special note: If you have just opened this book and turned to these plans, please be aware that they do not stand alone and need to be understood in the context of the ethos and principles explained in the text. Please be encouraged to read further for their full meaning.

Date	Leader	Helpers	Story/key point/starting point/questions/creative choices/ specific resources/song/book/image	Team's ideas
December, 1st Sunday			**Story:** God's son Jesus is born. **Key point:** Jesus was a real baby. **Starting point:** Get real, newest baby in session with its mum or dad. Discuss together what babies need. **Questions:** Ask parent of baby if they would like to give birth in a stable. How do you look after a baby? What does a baby need? What does a baby wear? **Creative choices:** Create stable on small (builders tray) or large scale with pretend/real donkey, sheep, cow etc. **Specific resources:** Create a manger for the dolls. Baby dolls, male and female, for role play e.g. bathing, feeding, putting to bed in manger (remember to encourage boys as well as girls to play with baby dolls as they need to learn to be good, nurturing dads). Swaddling clothes. **Song:** **Book/Image:**	
December, 2nd Sunday			**Story:** Angels tell shepherds. Visit Jesus in stable. **Key point:** Good news shouted from heaven. Which baby? **Starting point:** Whisper game of good news. Whisper: "I've got some chocolate! Pass it on!" (some will not hear/be able to pass on), say it slightly louder, and slightly louder till everyone has passed round and hears. Then share chocolate (NB allergies) God had good news and wanted to say it loudly...used angels.	

Special note: If you have just opened this book and turned to these plans, please be aware that they do not stand alone and need to be understood in the context of the ethos and principles explained in the text. Please be encouraged to read further for their full meaning.

Date	Leader	Helpers	Story/key point/starting point/questions/creative choices/ specific resources/song/book/image	Team's ideas
			OR: Guessing game; tray with variety of farm animals laid out. Leader says "I am thinking of an animal…it has four legs…a swishy tail…hooves…and an udder! Can you guess what it is?" The children can call out during any of the pauses if they want to guess which animal it is. Keep modelling how the game works or let children take turns when they understand the process.	
			God had to be sure the shepherds knew which baby was his son and so he was the only baby in a manger in Bethlehem.	
			Questions: How do you think the shepherds felt when they saw the angels? What do you think the angels looked like? I wonder, what might it have sounded like when they all sang? What do you think Joseph and Mary thought when the shepherds came into the stable?	
			Creative choices: Nativity figures for free play, builder's tray. Dressing up clothes for shepherds and angels, baby paraphernalia. Role play in the stable.	
			Specific resources: Variety of robust nativity figures that can be played with using builder's tray with stable resources/fields, angels and shepherds. Dressing up clothes. Manger.	
			Song:	
			Book/Image:	
December, 3rd Sunday			**Story:** Wise men/kings visit Jesus and bring presents.	
			Key point: Wise men/kings brought presents to Jesus. We can tell Jesus what we would like to give.	
			Starting point: Place selection of hats in the middle of the circle under a sheet so that the shape shows through. Ask children to guess what kind of hat it is and who might wear it. Make sure one of them is a crown. Lead into to story of kings and giving presents to Jesus.	

Special note: If you have just opened this book and turned to these plans, please be aware that they do not stand alone and need to be understood in the context of the ethos and principles explained in the text. Please be encouraged to read further for their full meaning.

Date	Leader	Helpers	Story/key point/starting point/questions/creative choices/ specific resources/song/book/image	Team's ideas
			Questions: I wonder, what sort of a hat could this be?... Who might wear this sort of a hat?... Why might they wear it?... I expect Mary and Joseph were a bit surprised at the special presents they gave Jesus...I wonder, what would you like to give him?	
			Creative choices: Dressing up as kings and queens. Dressing up nativity role play. Make sure of equal male and female grand clothes. Using all the hats to further their play. Add to gluing choices: glitter and sparkly jewels, diamond shaped sticky paper.	
			Specific resources: Variety of hats, some familiar to children: riding hat, workman's hard hat, wooly hat, motorbike helmet, baby's cap, peaked cap, crown.	
			Song:	
			Book/Image:	
December, 4th Sunday			**FAMILY SERVICE**	
			Creative choices: All come dressed as nativity characters.	
			Christmas Break	

ALLERGIES: Make sure the whole team are reminded about any children's allergies with reference to food etc.

Feely bag: An opaque, fabric bag with a drawstring top into which objects of interest can be placed. Children can then put their hand through the top of the bag in order to feel and guess what might be inside.

Builder's tray: A large, octagonal, heavy-duty tray on which builders mix cement. Here it is useful for containing sand, peat, stones, a little water and vegetation so that children can gather round and interact with the materials.

Special note: If you have just opened this book and turned to these plans, please be aware that they do not stand alone and need to be understood in the context of the ethos and principles explained in the text. Please be encouraged to read further for their full meaning.

Creative suggestions

Here are some other ideas that have worked well for us in the past and could be helpful.

Circle games

Both of these games can be adapted to fit the theme of a session, but they are also highly enjoyable for their own sakes. There are no winners or losers, just taking turns.

Giant, giant, who's got the keys?

The group sits in a circle and one child curls up in a ball pretending to be asleep… but their ears are awake! Next to them is a bunch of keys. When the giant is asleep, the leader points at a child in the circle who quietly gets up and tiptoes to the keys and carries them back to their place in the circle and sits down, hiding the keys behind their back. All the rest of the group also hide their hands behind their backs and we chant together, "Giant, giant, who's got the keys?" in a singsong voice.

The giant wakes up and looks round the circle and has three guesses as to who is hiding the keys.

So the leader asks, "Who do you think it is?"

The child points. The leader verbalizes: "Is it Joel?"

Joel then shows his empty hands. All chorus: "No! It's not Joel."

The child points again. "Is it Shashi?"

Chorus: "No! It's not Shashi." (Empty hands shown again.)

"Is it Oliver?" (Empty hands shown again.)

"No! It's not Oliver."

Leader: "Who was it?"

The child who did take the keys takes them out from behind their back and shakes them. All clap and say, "Well done!"

The child who did take the keys now has a turn as the giant.

If the giant guesses before the final reveal, then everybody claps and says, "Well done!"

The game ends when you want it to.

The bear and the honey pot

The procedure for this game is exactly the same as above, only this time it is a bear and the honey pot is a jar with bells in.

This time the bear is told to go to sleep with this rhyme:

> *Isn't it funny*
> *how a bear likes honey?*
> *Buzz, buzz buzz,*
> *I wonder why he does?*
> *Go to sleep, little bear.*

The bear goes to sleep. The leader then points to a child who quietly gets up, tiptoes to the bear, picks up the honey pot, returns to their place and puts the pot behind them. Everybody puts their hands behind them, pretending they have the pot. Together we say:

> *Wake up, little bear!*
> *Your honey pot's not there!*

Once again the person in the middle has three guesses (see above), and so the game continues.

Drama

With this age group drama is something that everyone can enter into at the same time, as it is not a performance for an audience, just for the participants. You need to model entering into every part to make sure all the adults join in.

Obviously, children who are reticent should not be pushed to conform, as they have a right to make that choice.

For example, with the story of the prodigal son, we can act the whole story: the son greedily asking for money; and then the father being sad; and the son eventually feeding the pigs (with some of the children being the pigs!). Make sure that you swap everyone round during the telling so that all get a chance to step into others' shoes. Here I have asked a strong adult to be the father forgiving the son so that the children can run into their arms to be swung round and feel the welcome home.

Likewise, with David and Goliath, I have asked a tall adult to stand on a chair and have draped them in long clothes so that they appear to be standing on the ground, so as the children look upwards they get some real idea of how gigantic Goliath was.

Music, singing and dance

There is a tremendous wealth of music, songs and dance that will vary over the world and arise out of the cultures and influences of the times. It is not possible to explore the wide range of different approaches here, but they need to reflect the local community. However, the principles remain the same – respecting children means that they:

- need to be given the highest quality opportunities in every genre
- need to be given the freedom to respond in their own unique way
- need competent adults who can sensitively engage with them through the different media
- need to have developmentally appropriate opportunities.

Puppets

I have seen puppets used brilliantly, and terribly as well! However, used well, they do seem to have a magical effect on children. To be good, they certainly need to be practised in front of a mirror and have a persona that is a character in its own right, rather than some patronizing, twee, babyish expression. Persona dolls have been used to good effect in some schools to help explore issues around emotional literacy. Although *Sesame Street* used puppets years ago, in my view they are still amongst the best, and address feelings and behaviour as well as learning in other areas in a relevant way for children, and in a non-patronizing manner.

A school colleague had a child in her class who was an elective mute (he chose not to speak at all during school time but spoke normally at home), and all sorts of strategies were employed to try to help him get over this hurdle – to no avail. However, one day he walked into school with his own puppet, stood in front of the whole class and addressed the class through the persona of the puppet! This was his solution and served as an important stepping-stone to communicating confidently at school.

A light box or an overhead projector

A brilliant use of an overhead projector (OHP) is to introduce it into the session maybe by telling a story using silhouettes of the characters and projecting them onto a wall or a hanging sheet. Interest is immediately focused. This then needs to be left for the children's individual experimentation with the opaque shapes, whilst allowing the story to be revisited as well. However, there are then endless fascinating possible developments: using found objects such as leaves, stones, shells, buttons, play jewellery, feathers or transparent plastic pieces, plastic bottles with different coloured water inside. Play like this can be captivating as it is dynamic, easily manipulated and non-prescriptive.

Another method is to use the OHP to shine its light onto a sheet with the children viewing from the other side of the sheet for shadow puppet play. Again, a lot of participation and investigation is provoked because it is so engaging and allows plenty room for individual creative expression.

If this or other ideas are hard to visualize, then there are some beautiful photographic booklets produced by Liz Buckler that are helpful.[5]

Ideas for releasing children's mark-making creativity

With all of the following ideas it is essential that you try them out beforehand, as subtle differences, for example, in the paint consistency, can make all the difference between a satisfying experience and a frustrating one for the children.

Once again, it is the process that is important and not the end product.

If there is to be an end product, it needs to be decided by the child. Regardless of the story suggested by the programme, I always offer a range of creative choices through which children can express their own ideas. Needless to say, aprons on top of play clothes should be used!

Wax resist

Using wax crayons on white paper encourages the children to explore any mark-making they want to. Then provide Brusho dye[6] to give a strong, thin paint colour, which can be used to wash over the whole picture. The wax shows through brightly as it pushes away the watery paint. As the colours of the diluted dye are strong, the effect can be stunning.

Squash-outs

Mix paint with some flour to thicken. Provide different sizes of paper that have been folded but are now open. Encourage the children to blob paint on one side, then refold the paper along the crease. Then encourage them to press hard while they smooth the paint that is now between the two sides. Carefully open the folded paper to reveal an amazing symmetrical image. Ask them what they can "see" in the picture. Use different coloured paints for interesting colour mixing.

String pulls

Provide paper that has been folded but is now open. Obtain some absorbent string and cut pieces the same length as the children's arms (approximately). Tie the string at one end to the middle of a pencil or a similar-sized piece of doweling. Mix runny paint in a pot and push the length of string in and leave it suspended by the pencil that now lies across the top of the paint pot. To create the effect, holding the pencil, lift the now soggy string out of the paint and coil it on one side of the paper. Fold the other piece of paper over the top and hold down. Whilst pressing down, pull the string out. Carefully open the paper to reveal an unusual symmetrical image which can prompt imaginative discussion. The string can be used again without dipping into the paint, as the string will have absorbed the paint and so can give more interesting images. Obviously different colour paints can be used which might result in colour mixing. Although this technique requires quite a lot of coordination, I have been able to support three-year-olds through to independent use of this ingenious method of applying paint.

Chalk drawing

Provide a range of coloured sugar paper and chalks of various colours. As they are soft to draw with, the children do not need to press very hard to produce a satisfying effect on the paper.

Chalk drawing on a blackboard is also a satisfying medium.

Fruit and vegetable printing

Choose two each of different kinds of fruit or vegetable that are available and cut them once along different axes. For example, an apple cut straight down produces a beautiful outline shape that we readily identify as an apple, whereas when it is cut horizontally, the seed casing produces a wonderful star shape in the middle of a circle. Onions horizontally cut have the lovely ring effect and even lemons produce surprisingly good prints. Cauliflower or broccoli florets produce brilliant prints when they are cut longitudinally.

Enjoy experimenting yourself. It is always important to try out the paint consistency first. Also use shallow trays for the paint so the fruit or vegetables can fit in. Sometimes the first print has too much paint on and so is best done on spare newspaper, and then the next few prints can be done directly on the cloth or other surface. I have used an old sheet of cotton and spread it over the table so that several children at once can enjoy printing, and then the fabric can be kept as a backdrop or drape.

There is something about a shared piece of work that helps to bring cohesion to the group and enables children to feel that they belong. Otherwise smaller pieces of fabric can be cut beforehand for individual expressions.

Texture printing (including crêpe paper)

Hunt round for objects with interesting surfaces and try dipping them in paint and printing with them. Then provide the children with a wide range from which to make their choices. Some suggestions are: toy cars, wooden blocks, clingfilm in scrunched-up balls of different sizes, cutlery, Lego, felt, leaves, shells, sticks, stones, buttons. Try using different coloured paper for different effects. I have also used torn pieces of crêpe paper, as the dye in the paper dissolves in water. So scrunch up a piece of crêpe paper and dip it in water and then print on white paper. The dye will also stain fingers for a while, but using some clear plastic gloves can protect the hands. I am generally used to having prettily coloured fingers and don't give it a second thought, and the parents of my children are fine with that too. However, you might want to check it out first!

Mono print

Add flour to thicken the paint and spread on a large shallow dish or tray. Use fingers for a wonderful tactile experience. If a child shows an interest in their mark-making, then gently lie a sheet of paper on the top, pressing lightly, then lift it up and a mono print image is captured.

Art Roc

This is also known as mod roc and is fabric impregnated with plaster of Paris. It used to be used to set broken limbs. This is a good modelling medium as it sets quickly and is fairly immediate and therefore appropriate for this age group.

Cut the art roc up into small squares, approximately 4 cm by 4 cm, and provide water in shallow trays. Offer a range of small junk materials such as cardboard, cylinders, boxes and wood off-cuts. The art roc is made moist by dipping in the water and is then smoothed over chosen shapes, or just arranged. As it will dry in a few minutes, the surface can then be painted or spattered.

Spatter painting

Put thin paint into a shallow tray. Using an old toothbrush, dip into the paint. Hold the brush horizontal to the paper or object on the table, face down, and stroke your index finger back along the bristles. As the bristles flick back, so does the paint, creating a satisfying spray effect. Remember to put lots of newspaper down and wear aprons!

Recycled modelling

Collect packaging, buttons, fabric and other materials that might be seen as junk and arrange them in *separate* containers to make them tempting to use, and from which the children can make their selections. They can then assemble their creations using glue, string and other joining mechanisms. These models can be painted or covered in art roc or just kept as they are.

Wood modelling, glue and nails

Off-cuts of wood and wood shavings can also be added to the recycled modelling choices to add variation and texture. With appropriate adult supervision, bring in real tools such as a hammer and nails, saws and hand-drills, and support the children as they enjoy using woodwork skills on soft wood such as pine or balsa. I have organized sessions like this with numerous nursery children and also in children's church, and they have loved being like Noah and his family, and Jesus and his!

Blow painting

Using strong, thin paint or brusho dye, mix up a selection of colours. Using a straw, dip the end into the dye, and place your finger over the top to create suction. Then hold the straw over the paper and lift off your finger. The dye will drop onto the paper. Now use the straw to blow down and chase the drops over the sheet of paper. The effect looks like winter trees but can be used in many ways. Again, I have been able to teach this technique successfully to three-year-olds onwards.

Icing-sugar effects

Mix icing sugar with water and spread thinly over a small piece of card. Then, using the same method as in blow painting, drop the dye on the icing sugar. The droplet will spread out in a delicate and beautiful way.

Weaving

I have used some plastic garden netting as the background through which to weave myriad materials. I have hung the netting at children's height down to the floor so that they can stand and comfortably reach it. In Bristol we have a scrap store which recycles the end products of industry, and being a city where hot-air balloons are made, there is a ready supply here of strips of fabric that the children love to weave with. I have also provided the weaving outside so that the children gather natural materials such as ivy and leaves and use those to weave into a tapestry with fabric, wool, straws and other found materials. This is really only a basic starting point, as there is so much that can be expressed in this way, including the use of photographs and significant objects, on a small as well as a large scale.

Clay

Out of the earth the first person was fashioned, and clay is a very basic, comfortable material to work with. Like water and sand, it is a continuous material that has unique properties. Just playing with it can be comforting and cathartic. It holds our fingerprints and so is very personal. Most children find it easy to engage with immediately, although there are some who are worried about getting "dirty". This can usually be overcome by providing a bowl of warm water, soap and a towel which they can use independently, so they can be confident of getting clean again. As always, children's choices need to be respected. Give each interested child a small lump to explore and experiment with. Later materials or tools can be added so that more effects can be created. Remember that if there is to be an end product, it needs to be decided by the child alone. The greatest challenge with clay is its storage, as it is bulky and needs to be kept moist, but it is worth it.

Ice balloons

Preparation is needed the day before. Fill some balloons with water by fixing the opening onto the nozzle of the tap, and gently turn the tap on until the balloon is fairly full. You might want to wear an apron just in case it all spurts out! Then tie a knot in the end and put it in the freezer overnight. Remove them from the freezer about an hour before they are needed and wrap them in newspaper. Place the balloons in a plastic tray or one in each, if you have several. Ask the children to feel and guess what could possibly be inside, along with lots of other questions prompting them to reflect on previous experiences or their imagination. Then let them unwrap the balloons, which might trigger more creative thinking.

I usually then offer some salt to sprinkle on top and get them to listen closely. Pinging sounds can be heard which are actually the ice cracking. Also the salt creates little rivulets as it lowers the freezing point of water, and so the ice melts around the salt granules. To demonstrate this more clearly, I use food dye, applying it with a straw used as a dropper, as described in "Blow painting" above. The dye runs down the channels and cracks created by the salt. It looks amazing and each one is unique. Often there is dramatic colour mixing as well.

You might well ask, "What is the point of doing this?"

Well, it often provokes a response of awe and wonder, which is not easy to create. Is it art? Is it science?

It is also valuable for its own sake and engages the children, triggering important discussions.

Many things can be used as a mould for freezing water (e.g. plastic gloves!), and even just blocks can be frozen with an object inside which gradually melts, revealing its treasure. This can be used to start a story. It can be left through the session in the water-play area.

God has made an amazing world and water is an incredible substance that can be explored and enjoyed.

Framing

When a child wants their picture or image to be kept, framing is an excellent way of celebrating that work. Framing actually tricks our eye and draws the viewer into the image. We are used to horizontal and longitudinal lines in our environment and that is why our perception is altered by a frame. I have managed to source mounts by going to a framing shop and asking for their redundant mounts, which I have been able to buy very cheaply. Then I simply attach the image to the back of the mount and then hang it. Where this is hung is also important. Celebrating work by framing it gives powerful messages to the artist and in this case, the child artist. It says, "I see what you have made and I value it… I respect your work as equal to adults' framed work…"

Those of you who have had your work displayed will know the powerful impact it has on your self-esteem when others respond positively to your work on display. Remember that it is not just "pictures" that can be displayed. Any of the techniques above, with the exception of the ice balloons, can be honoured in this way. Equality needs to be remembered and so, over time, every child's work should be displayed, provided they give permission.

An individual session plan

- Before the start of a session, I pray with the team for the children. I also follow the example of the little boy with the loaves and fishes who gave the little he had to Jesus, who made it enough to more than satisfy all who had come,[7] and pray that Jesus would take our preparations and our interactions and make them enough for his precious children that day. I also pray that he would fill us with his Spirit to truly welcome his children and that they would feel safe and loved.

- We provide juice and chopped-up fruit for the children as they arrive, remembering those with allergies, and come and sit in a circle on cushions.

- Sometimes there is catching-up conversation with the children. Then I lead into the starting point for the session, which needs to be something that hooks their interest – a fascination trap. I often use an object hidden in a bag for the children to feel and guess what it could be.

> For example, with the story of the lost coin, I put my teddy in a pillowcase and asked the children to guess what was inside. The point of the guessing is not to be "right" but to encourage the children to use their imaginations. I gave clues: "It is something that is precious to me..." Whatever the children guessed, I gave the same sort of answer: "It could be..." When the big reveal at the end happened, all were delighted and I talked about why the teddy was special to me and when I liked to cuddle him. Many joined in with stories of their special comforters. Then I linked it to the woman who lost a very special coin that was precious to her.

- The story is then explored in as engaging a way as possible. This can last between ten and fifteen minutes, depending on the children and what has been expected of them during church that morning.

- After that, I verbally offer the wide range of choices available, and the children make their initial decisions of where they will start engaging in play, either verbally or pointing. The adults then join in with their selections and focus solely on the children.

- This carries on for the remainder of the session, which might be for another hour.

- Towards the end of the session the children join us in tidying up.

- I hand over the children to their parents at the end with positive communication and observations of their children's interests.

- As we finish clearing up, I reflect with the team as to how well the session went, how to improve upon it, noticing children's interests and suggesting ideas to try another time. I also make sure I am specific in my appreciation of the support the team have given me.

Jesus told amazing spiritual truths using everyday concepts and created stories starting with the world of his listeners. We need to know our children well so that we can meet them where they are, at their starting point. For example, the concept of a picnic might be fairly universal, but for some it will mean a plastic bag with some sandwiches and a can of fizzy drink, but for others it might mean a hamper with a checked tablecloth and cutlery, and for still others it might mean a wider family event over a barbecue. We are there to connect with unique children and so we need to be genuinely respectful to make sure that the messages of the Bible are culturally relevant to them.

Reflection

- What is my favourite Bible story?
  - *What is the distilled essence of it that touches me?*
  - *How can I make this relevant to a three- to four-year-old?*
  - *How can I make this relevant to a five- to seven-year-old?*
- What is my favourite activity or hobby?
  - *How can I share this with my group of children?*
- Is there somebody I know who has a special interest or talent that I could invite to share with the group?

Isaiah 11:6

The wolf will live with the lamb,
the leopard will lie down with the goat,
the calf and the lion and the yearling together;
and a little child will lead them.

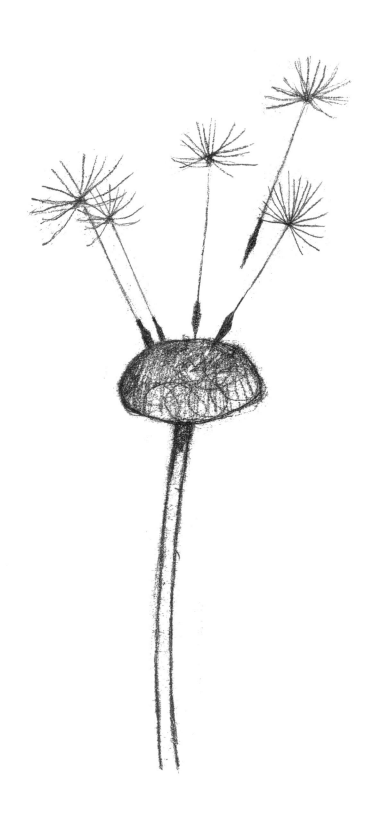

Epilogue

This last section will provide suggestions as to how to continue the discourse of this book and make it relevant to *your* children in *your* church at *this* time.

CHAPTER 13

The Time of Their Lives!

Over to you!

Isobel and Carrie

This book has been part of an ongoing dialogue – not a recipe book, nor a manual. We hope that you have been inspired to get to know the children you work with better through reading about the changing context of children's lives, the emerging research on child development and the playful nature of children. We also hope that you will have a deeper understanding of God's perspective of his church and the importance of the individual child in each church – and the rich qualities they can bring to church life.

In this book we have explored various themes and principles. We consider that respect is critically important in establishing positive and meaningful relationships with children and their families. This involves developing good listening skills, tuning in to the child and hearing their many languages and actively listening to their parents. We need to learn to see life though the eyes of the child. Although we acknowledge the uniqueness of each child, we know that we cannot be involved in a very young child's life without being involved with their family and immediate community. Our view of relationships is that they are multi-layered and critical for our well-being and spiritual health. Young children will develop their understanding of God as a Father through the relationships they establish with key people in their lives.

And you are their key people in church – a place they may well connect with God.

> Evie was just two years old when her great-grandma died. She attended the funeral in the chapel of the nursing home. During the service, Evie asked me where great-grandma was. Before I could answer, she asked me where Jesus was. I replied, "Everywhere." "No," said Evie and asked me again. I clearly didn't get the answer right. When I told her mum about this episode, she said that I should have answered, "He's in you and he's in me." This was based on a song in crèche at church and has become a regular question and answer that Evie likes to have with her mum!

Children in the Way?

This relationship with parents is so important. We hope that you have found some of the ideas for involving parents and communicating with them helpful. Visiting a "Stay and Play" group for parents and children under three years, it was interesting to note how parents would openly talk about seemingly minor incidents with their children which were causing them concern. Just a few suggestions or an empathetic listener was all the parents needed to help them come to their own conclusions or make decisions to deal with their concerns. So often, when I have been in a crèche in different churches, I have had similar conversations with parents. Supporting the parents will support them in their nurture of their children and in turn, the child's relationship with God.

We have argued that children are competent as learners, well able to explore and make sense of their own world. We have suggested the types of stimulating environments for children from birth to seven years old, proposing that these should contain fascination traps to inspire the children and engage them in deep learning experiences. Our view is that young children learn through play that is sensory and purposeful.

Sensory, because children use their senses from birth, as tools for survival initially and then increasingly as tools for exploration and innovation.

And purposeful, because the child has chosen what they want to do, which is meaningful to them.

We also believe that children are creative beings, made in the image of God, with creativity woven into their DNA. We have explored the connection that creativity has with learning and thinking and we have described ways of providing spaces for children's creativity to flourish and resources that inspire and release, as opposed to those that inhibit and shut down. We have made explicit what quality looks like at these earliest years in a child's life and the benefit to the whole church of making children a high priority and a worthwhile investment.

We have also discussed the importance of using the medium of Bible stories for children of all ages, but prepared appropriately for each age group. We considered how stories allow children to imagine and think freely. They enable the child to have time to process their thoughts, relate the story to their own experiences, then repeat or re-enact the events to understand the concepts within a context. This is why it is so important to have the children's own experiences as a starting point.

Like you, we believe that children need to feel safe and secure, happy, valued and welcomed.

Like you, we enjoy children and the colour they bring to our lives with their laughter and fun, their playfulness and expressive language and their innate connection with God. But life is not all rosy for them and they need sensitive, responsive yet playful adults. If we are to understand them, we need to keep developing our knowledge of young children and the context of growing up in the twenty-first century.

Developing a reflective approach to our work with very young children and communicating well within our teams, will build confidence and convey confidence to the parents and children in our groups.

Our own relationship with God is a priority.

How can we hope to nurture the very youngest children in their spiritual development if we don't nurture our own? No doubt you have become even more aware of the immense responsibility, as well as the privilege, of working with very young children in church, so it is essential that we make sure that our own spiritual needs are being met. We need to look after ourselves and ensure that we have a support network.

So, now it is over to you!

So, what next?

There's no time like the present… and the present is the only time we have.

So, take a moment now to step back and do some blue-sky thinking.

By this I mean go to a place, physically or mentally and spiritually, and let your thoughts flow without constraint as you envisage the good things you would like to provide for your church children.

Imagine you could change anything. What would you do?

Capture as much as you can of this in written form.

Now use the headings below as prompts to trigger further thinking:

- Who would you need to talk to?
- What space would you like to develop?
- What resources would you like to provide?
- Who would you like in your team?
- Who would be able to support you?

Remembering the "circles of reflection", using that methodology and keeping the children in focus, begin to prioritize the most significant things first. Sometimes the urgent issues shout louder than the important ones, like an incessant telephone demanding to be picked up, but concentrate instead on the truly vital matters.

Now divide your prioritized list into short-term and long-term plans.

Choose one short-term plan and itemize carefully the small steps you need to take in order to achieve it. This is a personalized version of "Who will do what by when?" It could even be something as simple as arranging a time to share your thinking with somebody who might be able to support you.

Repeat the process for a long-term plan. This will have many more steps in it and may involve engaging others to share your goal for the children.

Keep records of your thinking so that later on, not only can you reflect on the distance you have travelled, but also you can keep in mind your vision for the future, for times when you cannot see the wood for the trees.

We hope that you have been able to add your voice to ours through the course of this book. You will have noticed the dandelion images at the beginning of each section and will remember why we chose this symbol. Hopefully those dandelion seeds will have dispersed far and wide to where you are. Perhaps your journal looks like ours, with more questions than answers, but lots of ideas.

It has been our intention to work alongside you to enable you to reflect on your work with children and plan innovatively, whatever your starting point may be.

Drawing on proven academic research, and years of personal experience, we hope that *Children in the Way?* has been a highly practical book for you. We have sought to have a clear emphasis on quality provision for children and what this looks like at different ages from birth to seven. What we have covered has obvious implications for those working with children of all ages, and even for those interested in mission and church growth.

This book is not a final statement but part of the ongoing dialogue that continually takes place as further research reveals new insights into child development and our increasing revelation of children's spirituality, which then merges with different church cultures and individual children.

We need to keep seeking further revelation of God's perspective through the Holy Spirit for *our* particular children at *this* time, in *this* church.

Whilst remembering, of course, that each child is a unique individual.

Maybe you have been challenged through some of the concepts and ideas and feel the weight of responsibility for bringing about change in your children's church. Although there is immense responsibility with these ones who are close to God's heart, also a tremendous privilege and joy come through working with our youngest children.

Writing this book has been like giving birth to a vision that is important to both of us. Like giving birth, our interest in you does not stop here!

This is not the end of the book, as we would like to continue this dialogue with you. See it as more like a comma than a full stop!

If you would like us to work with your team in some way, do contact us, as we would be willing to come and share ideas or lead workshops and even travel abroad.[1]

The focus of this book has been children, the message of this book is for adults and the vision of this book is that you will make a positive difference to the children in your church.

Give them the time of their lives!

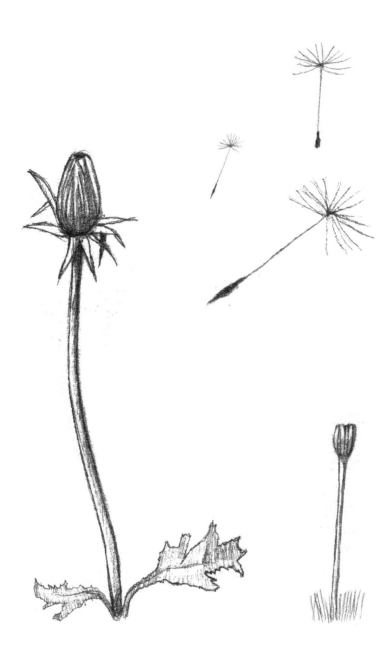

References

Chapter 1: Time Flies

1. Goldschmied, Elinor, and Jackson, S., *People under three: Young children in daycare*, 2nd edition, London: Routledge, 2004.
2. Matthew 18:3 NIV.
3. Matthew 19:14 NIV.
4. A Criminal Records Bureau check investigates the individual and checks whether they have had any criminal convictions. To have a CRB check means the person has not been convicted by the law courts. At the time of going to press, the rules regarding who has to be checked in the UK are changing. Whatever the legal framework, the children's best interests need to come first.
5. Esther 4:14 NIV.

Chapter 2: Just in Time?

1. Luke 9:48 NRSV.
2. Matthew 18:10 NIV.
3. Mark 10:14–16 NRSV.
4. Chugani, Harry, "Positron Emission Tomography", in *Rethinking the Brain: New Insights into Early Development*, ed. Rima Shore, New York: Families and Work Institute, 1997.
5. Brotherton, Sean, *Understanding Brain Development in Young Children*, NDSU Extension Service, BrightBeginnings #4, 2005.
6. Shore, Rima, ed., *Rethinking the Brain: New Insights into Early Development*, New York: Families and Work Institute, 1997.
7. *All our Futures,* Department for Education and Employment (DfEE), 1999. Quotation from Lord Stone of Blackheath, Managing Director of Marks and Spencer.
8. Matthew 18:1–4 NRSV.

Chapter 3: Quality Time

1. "The rule of first mention" when studying the Bible, means that the first time a word or phrase is mentioned usually gives the key to its meaning in other places in the Bible.
2. Shore, Rima, ed., *Rethinking the Brain: New Insights into Early Development*, New York: Families and Work Institute, 1997.
3. Chugani, Harry, "Positron Emission Tomography", in *Rethinking the Brain: New Insights into Early Development*, ed. Rima Shore, New York: Families and Work Institute, 1997. *Synaptic Density:* Synapses are created with astonishing speed in the first three years of life. For the rest of the first decade, children's brains have twice as many synapses as adults' brains.
4. Pert, Candace, *The Molecules of Emotion*, Scribner USA, 1997; Simon & Schuster UK, 1998.
5. Shore, Rima, ed., *Rethinking the Brain: New Insights into Early Development*, New York: Families and Work Institute, 1997.
6. Carl Jung (1875–1961), Swiss Psychologist. http://www.quotationspage.com/quotes/Carl_Jung

7. *All our Futures*, DfEE, 1999, http://www.cypni.org.uk/downloads/alloutfutures.pdf (22.02.11).

8. Tele-seminar interview between Sally Goddard Blythe and Pinky McKay on the importance of physical interaction in the early years http://www.sallygoddardblythe.co.uk/index.php (07.02.11).

9. Goddard Blythe, Sally, *The Well Balanced Child*, Stroud: Hawthorn Press, 2003; *What Babies and Children REALLY Need*, Stroud: Hawthorn Press, 2008; *Attention, Balance and Co-ordination – the A,B,C of Learning Success*, Chichester: Wiley-Blackwell, 2009.

10. Goddard Blythe, Sally, Institute for Neuro-Physiological Psychology, abridged extract from *Natural Parent* magazine, January/February 1999.

11. Bruce, Tina, *Early Childhood Education*, 3rd edition, London: Hodder Arnold, 2005, p. 59.

Poem: "The Little Boy"

1. Buckley, Helen, "The Little Boy", first published in *School Arts Magazine*, October 1961, http://home.bresnan.net/~cabreras/theboy.htm (10.01.11).

Chapter 4: Past Times

1. Maslow, A. H., "A Theory of Human Motivation", *Psychological Review*, 50(4), 1943, pp. 370–96.

2. http://www.suite101.com/content/how-maslows-hierarchy-of-needs-affects-children-a243718

3. Layard, Richard and Dunn, Judy, *A Good Childhood: Searching for values in a competitive age*, London: Penguin, 2009.

4. Alexander, R., ed., *Children, their world, their education: Final report and recommendations of the Cambridge Review*, London: Routledge, 2010.

5. NRSV.

6. Bronfenbrenner, U., *The Ecology of human development: Experiments by nature and design*, Cambridge, MA: Harvard University Press, 1979.

Chapter 5: Changing Times

1. 1 Corinthians 12:12–27.

2. Thank you, Jim Graham.

3. Genesis 1:27 NRSV.

4. See Chapter 10.

5. Rodd, Jillian, *Leadership in Early Childhood*, 3rd edition, Open University Press, 2005.

6. Matthew 18:1–4.

7. Luke 9:1, 2.

8. Luke 24:13–35.

9. Davies, Elspeth, Bristol Early Years Advisor.

10. http://www.iwise.com/James_Baldwin (22.01.11).

Chapter 6: Time Out!

1. Rees Larcombe, Jennifer, *Journey into God's Heart: The True Story of a Life of Faith*, Hodder and Stoughton, 2003.
2. Genesis 1:3 NIV.
3. Galatians 3:28 NIV.
4. 1 Corinthians 10:23 NIV.

Poem: "No Way. The Hundred Is There."

1. "The 100 languages of children", Loris Malaguzzi, Founder of the Reggio Emilia Approach, translated by Lella Gandini, www.chevychasereggio.com/poem.htm (15.11.10).

Chapter 7: Taking Time

1. Bowlby, 1969, http://www.simplypsychology.org/bowlby.html (24.02.11).
2. Gerhardt, S., *Why Love Matters: How affection shapes a baby's brain*, London: Routledge, 2004.
3. Schore, A., 1994, cited in Gerhardt, S., *Why Love Matters: How affection shapes a baby's brain*, London: Routledge, 2004.
4. In 2009/10, an estimated 9.8 million working days in Britain were lost through work-related stress. On average, each person suffering from work-related stress took an estimated 22.6 days off in 2009/10. http://www.hse.gov.uk/statistics/causdis/stress/days-lost.htm (28.01.11).
5. Gerhardt, S., *Why Love Matters: How affection shapes a baby's brain*, London: Routledge, 2004.
6. De Pree, M., *Dear Zoe*, San Francisco: HarperCollins, 1996.

Chapter 8: Play Time

1. Okri, Ben, *In Arcadia*, London: Weidenfeld & Nicholson, 2002.
2. *Te Whariki*, National Curriculum for Early Education in New Zealand, 1996, http://www.educate.ece.govt.nz/learning/curriculumAndLearning/TeWhariki.aspx (accessed 24.02.11).
3. Nye, R., *Children's Spirituality: What it is and why it matters*, London: Church House Publishing, 2009.
4. Henry Davies, William (1871–1940).
5. Gandini, L., in Edwards, C., Gandini, L. and Foreman, G., eds., *The Hundred Languages of Children*, London: Ablex Publishing, 1994, p. 149.
6. Paley, Vivian Gussin, *Walley's Stories*, Cambridge, MA: Harvard University Press, 1981.
7. Goldschmied, Elinor, *People Under Three*, 2nd edition, London: Routledge, 2004.
8. Strozzi, P., Guidici, C. and Rinaldi, C., eds., *Making Learning Visible: Children as Individual and Group Learners*, Italy: Reggio Children, 2001, p. 67.
9. "Curriculum Guidance in Oxfordshire", 1991, cited in Nutbrown, C. & Page, J.,*Working with Babies and Children from Birth to Three*, London: Sage, 2008, p. 172.
10. Nutbrown, Cathy, in Abbott, L. and Nutbrown, C., eds., *Experiencing Reggio Emilia: Implications for pre-school provision*, Open University Press, 2001, p. 112.

Poem: "What did you do at pre-school today?"

1. Heard, Sue, Staffordshire Pre-school Learning Alliance, 'What did you do at pre-school today?'

Chapter 10: Talking Time

1. Laevers, Ferre, EXE project, Leuven, Belgium, 1994.
2. Pascal, Chris, *Effective Early Learning Project*, University College Worcester, 1994.
3. 2 Corinthians 7:9.
4. www.highscope.org (19.01.11).
5. "Supporting children in resolving conflict", http://secure.highscope.org/productcart/pc/viewPrd.asp?idproduct=629 (18.08.11).
6. John 21:15–19.

Chapter 11: It's About Time!

1. HighScope Perry Preschool Study, http://www.highscope.org/Content.asp?ContentId=219 (20.01.11).
2. Pascal, Chris, *Effective Early Learning Project*, University College Worcester, 1994.
3. HighScope Perry Preschool Study, http://www.highscope.org/Content.asp?ContentId=219 (20.01.11).
4. Webster, V., Webster, A. with Kingston, C., *Supporting Learning in the Early Years*, Avec Designs, 1997.

Chapter 12: Once upon a Time...

1. Matthew 7:28–29.
2. Luke 18:25.
3. Matthew 13:1–9.
4. Matthew 7:9–12.
5. Buckler, L., *The Inspired Child*, info@mylittlebooks.co.uk
6. Brusho dye is a dry, powder, non-toxic dye, small amounts of which can be diluted with water to form an intense colour. Search the internet for the best stockists.
7. John 6:9.

Chapter 13: The Time of Their Lives!

1. Do contact us: http://www.childrenintheway.com